FAITH UNPLUGGED

STORIES FOR GUYS
TO CHALLENGE WHAT YOU BELIEVE AND HOW YOU LIVE

HONOR HB BOOKS

Inspiration and Motivation for the Seasons of Life

COOK COMMUNICATIONS MINISTRIES
Colorado Springs, Colorado • Paris, Ontario
KINGSWAY COMMUNICATIONS LTD
Eastbourne, England

Honor Books® is an imprint of
Cook Communications Ministries, Colorado Springs, CO 80918
Cook Communications, Paris, Ontario
Kingsway Communications, Eastbourne, England

FAITH UNPLUGGED: STORIES FOR GUYS TO CHALLENGE WHAT YOU BELIEVE
AND HOW YOU LIVE
© 2006 by Honor Books

Manuscript written by Jason Jackson
Cover Design: Zoë Tennesen-Eck Design
Cover Photo: ©JupiterImages, ©Photodisc (Getty Images) and ©Stockbyte Images

First Printing, 2006
Printed in the United States of America

3 4 5 6 7 8 9 10

All Scripture quotations, unless otherwise marked, are taken from *THE MESSAGE*.
Copyright © by Eugene H. Peterson 1993, 1994, 1995, 1996, 2000, 2001, 2002.
Used by permission of NavPress Publishing Group. Scripture quotations marked
NIV are taken from the *Holy Bible, New International Version®. NIV®*. Copyright ©
1973, 1978, 1984 by International Bible Society. Used by permission of
Zondervan. All rights reserved.

ISBN-13: 978-1-56292-709-7
ISBN-10: 1-56292-709-4

TABLE OF CONTENTS

Presented To:

_____

By:

_____

Date:

_____

INTRODUCTION

Guys tend to experience life through doing. We're people of action. We learn about life by doing things, exploring the world, and measuring ourselves against others—and ourselves. The way we live as Christians is much the same. We know that our faith isn't really faith unless it's lived, done, and experienced. We like to put our faith in action.

This book can help you do just that. Experience Faith Unplugged through these true-to-life stories of guys just like you, exploring not just what you believe, but also how you allow your beliefs to influence your every action and decision.

Explore how your faith works out in real-life situations that guys your age face every day: relating to friends who don't share your faith, making choices that are based on how God wants people to live, navigating the treacherous waters of popular culture as a believer, figuring out godly ways to relate to parents when they just don't get you, and just doing life from God's perspective. As you read about these situations, you can learn what faith means as you put it into action in your everyday life.

Each story also comes with life insights:

• **DOWNLOAD** gives you God's perspective about the situation in the story.

• **FAITH UNPLUGGED** is a simple rule of thumb to help you make wise decisions.

• **FAITH LINK** helps you begin dialogue with God honestly and clearly.

• **POWER UP** holds you accountable for your decisions and actions and helps you consider the bigger picture.

Faith Unplugged. It's an up close and personal understanding of who you are—and how your faith influences your actions in every situation. It's reality. Unfiltered. The tools you need to live the life of faith to its fullest!

100% CERTAINTY

Doubt

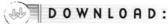

"I don't think the way you think. The way you work isn't the way I work." God's Decree. Isaiah 55:8

The voice wasn't loud. It wasn't even audible or external. It was like an idea that grabs your attention against your will. Or waking up one morning with an annoying song in your head that plays continuously in your mind for two years. Though the voice was faint, it often consumed and distracted. There were moments he found the ability to ignore its cries, but never the power to turn it off. The voice spoke loudest on Wednesdays, Sundays, and when he was alone.

It was the sound of doubt. It spoke in questions and in statements. "Is that really true? Is God real? Did Jesus live? Did Jesus die? Did Jesus rise again? Was Jesus really the Son of God, who said and did what his followers claim, or is he merely a legend whose glory increases with the passing of time? It's not true. God is a lie, a figment of your imagination. He can't hear you speak; stop pretending he can. If he existed, you would know it without a doubt; you could see him, touch him, hear him, experience him, but you never have, have you? And people who say they have can't prove it. No one can prove any of it."

For a few days, Mark considered the consequences of talking to Denny, his youth leader at church. *What if my questions mean that I'm not a Christian? Will he kick me out of church? Will he tell my parents? Will he tell the pastor? Will he tell the youth group—or make me tell them?* Mark imagined every response, spending extra time contemplating the worst-case scenarios. In the end, he decided to come forward. At least then, he might have some answers.

Mark called the church. "May I speak to Denny please?"

The phone rang briefly, and then: "Denny Wagoner."

"Um, hi, Denny ... this is, um, Mark ... Mark Rice from youth group. I was wondering, um ... I was wondering if I could, like, talk to you sometime about some stuff. If you're busy, um ... or you can't, it's OK ... but if ... if you can, it would be great."

Denny was just getting ready to leave, so he offered to take Mark out for ice cream later in the week. Mark reconsidered his decision numerous times. At one point, he thought about "calling in sick" instead of talking. But since Denny was picking Mark up at his house, Mark figured he'd better go.

It was the Wednesday afternoon before their weekly youth group meeting. Mark felt guilty for taking up Denny's time and thanked him for the ice cream about a hundred times. After their sundaes arrived, Denny asked why Mark wanted to meet.

"You mentioned on the phone that there was some stuff that you wanted to talk to me about, right?"

Mark paused, his spoon halfway to his mouth. "Yeah, well, I don't know if you remember this or not. Either way it doesn't matter. If you do, that's cool, but if not that's cool too," Mark said, trying to find a way to bring up his reason for meeting. He took a couple more spoonfuls of sundae, and then continued. "Anyway, when you talked about it, I thought maybe I could talk to you. I thought you might have some advice or know someone who has gone through the same thing." He continued to try to delay the inevitable. "So I called."

"OK, so what did I say that spurred all of this?" Denny said, hoping to help him along.

"Last Wednesday night, you said something about doubt. I don't remember exactly what you said, but it sounded like you knew someone who struggled with it."

"What kind of doubt are you struggling with, Mark?"

"All kinds, I guess, but mainly I doubt God," he answered quietly.

"Is it the kind of doubt where you question whether or not God will do something or is capable of doing that something? Or is it the kind of doubt where you question his existence, and therefore, everything else?" he inquired.

Mark paused. "Umm ... the second one."

"In that case, I do know someone."

"You do?" The realization that someone else wrestled

FAITH UNPLUGGED:

Questions are not the same as unbelief.

with the same uncertainty relieved him. Just knowing other people had the same questions helped Mark feel less alone. "Can I ask who?" he continued.

"Me," Denny replied. "In fact, I still deal with doubt."

"But how can that be? You're the youth leader, and you seem to know all the answers."

"Mark, being the youth leader doesn't make me perfect or change the fact that I'm a human being who struggles with different things."

"I know that. I guess I just think that people like you—in the church, I mean—have it all figured out."

"I've dealt with doubt ever since I became a Christian. Even before. I was the kind of person who questioned everything. My questions wore my parents and teachers out. For some reason, I needed to have answers, logical explanations or undeniable experiences to believe something was true. Accepting Jesus didn't remove my quizzical nature. Honestly, it made it worse."

"Why?"

"I wanted proof, I guess."

"What do you mean?"

"Just like when I was a kid, I wanted God to give me answers, logical explanations and undeniable experiences. Then I could be a hundred percent certain that he was real. But the life of faith doesn't offer that kind of certainty. Mark, when I looked for total assurance, what I really wanted was a God I could understand and control. I wanted a God I could fit into a box.

"But God is not that way. He is bigger than I can fathom and more profound than I could ever understand. The Bible describes it saying, 'His ways are not my ways, and his thoughts are not my thoughts.' I've finally figured out that God isn't someone we can understand completely, but he is someone we can trust completely. Trust is risky, especially for people like us. Trust is placing confidence in something other than ourselves or our ability to understand. God wants us to trust him. The assurance that faith brings comes from trusting that God is despite what we might think or feel."

"Whoa. That's really deep," Mark said, causing Denny to chuckle.

"I know. Sorry. I can get a little carried away," he added with a laugh. "Now, that doesn't mean that God wants us to live our lives with tormenting questions about how he isn't real. For me, I continually have to let go of my need to understand, to know, and to control."

"OK," Mark said. "So how do I do that?"

"Look, it sounds crazy, but you sort of have to trust God to help you with your doubt. I just ask God to help me see more of who he is and to help me with my doubts."

"So having doubts ... having doubts doesn't make me not a Christian?" Mark asked.

"No way," Denny told him. "It's OK to have questions about God or even wonder sometimes if he's real. But, instead of focusing on my doubts, I focus on God and remember all the great things God has done for me and for other people I know.

"Mark, just remember: God is big enough to handle your doubts, and if you keep turning to him, even in the midst of those doubts, you'll be on the right track."

 ## FAITH LINK:

Jesus, I deal with doubt. There are a lot of things I'm uncertain about in the arena of faith, but I'm learning that that's the point. The life of faith is learning to trust you completely—not facts, figures, or proofs. Help me trust you more.

 ## POWER UP:

Many Christians deal with doubt in some capacity. Doubt isn't the same as unbelief. Unbelief is refusing to believe and therefore the absence of faith. Doubt happens when one honestly strives to believe, and therefore faith exists. Do you doubt? What do you do with it? How you respond matters. The best responses to doubt will lead you toward trust and worship. The worst responses will lead you to unbelief. Commit to take your doubt to God. Ask him for help. Search the Bible for other faithful doubters and learn from their lives. If you have close Christian friends you can trust, tell them and ask them to pray for you as well.

HERE FOR YOU

Abandonment

DOWNLOAD:

A father to the fatherless, a defender of widows, is God in his holy dwelling. Psalm 68:5 NIV

Jermaine raced down the hallway to his third-period history class. Mr. Johnson was sitting at his desk in front of an empty room when Jermaine burst through the door. "Right on time," Mr. Johnson said, chuckling as he looked at the clock. These two-minute preclass conversations had become a daily ritual this semester.

"Hey, Mr. Johnson! How are you?"

"Good, and you?" he replied while moving from his chair to the edge of the desk.

"Awesome! I have some great news." Jermaine exhaled with a combination of relief and excitement.

"That's great. I have some news for you, too. You go first."

Mr. Johnson's response failed to reflect Jermaine's exuberance. Noticing his teacher's lackluster response, Jermaine insisted otherwise. "No, you first. We both know I usually end up doing all the talking."

"Well, if you insist ... Jermaine, I don't know exactly how to say this, but this is going to be my last semester teaching here at Hillcrest."

"What?!" Jermaine blurted. His expression changed from enthusiastic to horrified in a split second.

"I've accepted an offer to teach in Atlanta, where my wife's family lives. It'll mean a pay raise and we'll be closer to Sarah's parents when the baby is born." Mr. Johnson's wife was expecting their first child in September.

"But you can't move!" Jermaine's voice cracked. "You said you were going to be here for me, and now you're moving to Atlanta!" Jermaine couldn't find words for a moment as he wrestled with his emotions. Finally, his hurt turned to anger. "You know what? It doesn't matter; I don't need you anyway. I don't need anybody." He turned and ran from the room.

"Jermaine, wait a minute." Mr. Johnson stood, shocked and concerned. He knew his news would be hard for Jermaine to take, but he never expected such a strong reaction.

The two had developed a close relationship over the past eight months since Jermaine's father left his mother. Jermaine's father tried to comfort him at the time, saying, "Jermaine, this has nothing to do with you. This is between your mother and me. We're still going to see each other. You can come over on the weekends and I'll still be at all your school events. Nothing is going to change between us, OK? I'll be here for you. I promise."

Those words played like a scratched CD in Jermaine's mind. First his dad, and now Mr. Johnson. He figured that "I'll be here for you" meant about as much as a store clerk asking how he was doing. People say things like that because that's what they're supposed to say.

Jermaine had thought Mr. Johnson was different, but he was obviously wrong. *I'm never going to trust anyone again,* Jermaine swore silently as he looked for a place to be alone and plot out how to avoid Mr. Johnson for the rest of the semester.

Jermaine had not seen or heard from his father since he received a Christmas card in January postmarked from somewhere in New York. Instead of his father, it was Mr. Johnson who had become his biggest fan, attending all of his school functions, stopping to talk to him in the halls and before class, and even frequenting the local restaurant where Jermaine waited tables.

Their unexpected friendship had provided Jermaine with the help and encouragement he desperately needed. Now Jermaine was devastated. *What's the point of trusting anyone, when eventually they're going to leave? It's just not worth it.*

All day Mr. Johnson searched for Jermaine between classes and after school, but Jermaine was pretty good at making himself scarce. That evening Mr. Johnson shared the story with his wife over dinner. Sarah had become quite fond of Jermaine and had waited anxiously all day to hear about the conversation. "Then he stormed out of the room ..."

"Oh no! What did you do? Did you go after him?"

"Honestly, I didn't know what to do, so I just let him go. I was so shocked by his reaction that I froze. I knew this would be hard, but I didn't think it would be like this. I decided to give him some space and talk to him later, but he's doing everything he can to avoid me."

"Why don't you call his mother?" Sarah asked. "We could always go over there and talk with him."

"I guess it wouldn't hurt to try."

After dinner Mr. Johnson called Jermaine's mother, Sandra Washington. He was relieved when she answered the phone. After exchanging greetings, Jermaine's mom listened intently as Mr. Johnson explained the morning incident.

Jermaine hadn't said anything to his mom, but she knew something was wrong. He picked at his dinner, avoided her questions with short replies, and went to his room early. She had assumed it had something to do with his father, so she gave him some space.

"I looked for him the rest of the day," Mr, Johnson continued, "but I couldn't find him. I was wondering if my wife and I could come over tonight to speak with him."

"You most certainly can. Do you remember where we live?"

"Yes, and thank you so much. I don't know if this will help, but it's worth a try. We'll see you in a few minutes."

Twenty minutes later the doorbell rang. Jermaine ignored it until he heard a gentle tap on his door.

Great! She wants me to come out and meet another one of her stupid friends. Can't she tell that I'm in no mood for meaningless small talk? Jermaine thought as his mother tapped again and then quietly opened the door. "Jermaine?"

"What?" His answer seethed with frustration.

"Someone's here to see you."

"Who is it?"

"Mr. Johnson and his wife"

"What are they doing here? I don't want to talk to them."

"Listen here, young man. You get up off that bed this instant and come out here and hear what they have to say."

 FAITH UNPLUGGED:

God often reveals himself to us through the people he brings into our lives.

Reluctantly, Jermaine followed her to the living room.

"Hey, Jermaine."

"Mr. Johnson, Mrs. Johnson." Jermaine's eyes flicked toward them for a second and then refocused on the floor. He could barely look at the Johnsons, partly out of anger and partly out of embarrassment at his own reaction.

"Jermaine, I realize that my news came as quite the shock to you today. Before I say anything else, I want you to know that I'm sorry for the way our decision affects you. It wasn't an easy decision for us to make. One of the hardest parts of our decision was leaving you.

"You're an amazing kid. I enjoy being your teacher and I love being your friend. This might not mean much to you considering all you've been through with your dad, but I'm still going to be your friend. Sure things will change. It will be hard to sneak in our two-minute talks before third hour from Atlanta, but I'll be there for you. I can't talk to you about this at school, but I want you to know that I believe God brought me into your life and you into mine. I'm not about to turn my back on you. I hope that you'll allow me time to prove that to you. In the meantime, we're praying for you."

Jermaine stood silently with his hands in his pockets. After lingering for a few seconds, Mr. Johnson and his wife thanked Jermaine and Mrs. Washington for letting them stop over. They dismissed themselves as Jermaine sluggishly made his way back to his room. The words "God brought me into your life" echoed in his head. It had been a long time since he considered God. Would God be there for him, even if Mr. Johnson might not?

FAITH LINK:

Jesus, I feel abandoned. There have been people in my life who either promised to be there for me or should have been there, but for one reason or another they let me down. Please help me to forgive them and fill the space they left behind.

POWER UP:

Perhaps you have felt that someone close to you has abandoned you in some way. It could have been a parent, teacher, coach, pastor, sibling, or even a friend. Sometimes abandonment is physical, but other times people disconnect from you spiritually or emotionally. When someone leaves, you feel a range of emotions, including hurt, anger, and rejection.

Jesus himself felt the pain of abandonment. When he was arrested, his friends scattered and left him to face his toughest hours alone. He wants to help you not only deal with those emotions, but also fill the gaps created by their absence. Often Jesus fills those gaps personally. Other times, he brings people into your life to help. Recognize not only those people in your life, but God's involvement as well. Thank him and thank them for the role they play.

LIVE TO BE OLD

Parents

 **DOWNLOAD:**

"Honor your father and mother" is the first commandment that has a promise attached to it, namely, "so you will live well and have a long life." Ephesians 6:2-3

"I hope I never see him again!" Brian shouted, walking into his uncle's hardware store. Brian's dad had just dropped him off for work, and the two had had a knockdown argument. Again.

"Who?" Uncle Ron asked.

"Bruce!" Brian said.

"You mean your dad?"

"Yeah, my *dad*," Brian said, the word squeezed out between gritted teeth.

"Ah, yes," Uncle Ron said, with an understanding twinkle in his eye. He handed Brian a box cutter and gave instructions for stocking some shelves in the storeroom.

Brian and his father's strained relationship began years ago. When Brian was a young boy, his father, Bruce, worked incessantly at two jobs. Bruce set high financial goals for his family and strived to meet them. After his underprivileged childhood, he vowed his children would never experience the same. Bruce's primary occupation was sales, which translated into long hours of stressful commission-based work. He also worked part-time doing computer maintenance and repair, which he did late at night or early in the morning. Brian's father was rarely home. When he was home, he was tired and irritable, often yelling, most frequently at his oldest child, Brian:

"Brian, stop it!

"Brian, leave me alone! All I want is some peace and quiet.

"%*^(@#, Son. I'm trying to watch TV.

"Go help your mother.

"Get me a drink.

"No, I don't want to play. I've been working all day for this family. I'm tired and I just want to relax."

In Brian's early teen years, his relationship with his father went from strained to broken. Bruce landed a better job, which meant he only had to work one. But his hours hardly changed. Brian reasoned his dad liked being at work more than at home. Bruce was a much better employee than a father. As an employee, he was hardworking, reliable, independent, resourceful, inventive, dedicated, and a perfectionist.

But as a father, he was demanding, absent, disconnected, unresponsive, apathetic, indifferent, and a perfectionist. The only thing Bruce did more of than work was drink. The only thing he did more than drink was lecture.

In those years Bruce seemed to think parenting meant criticizing and correcting from the sideline. He no longer just yelled. Bruce yelled, reprimanded, and then instructed Brian on how he should act. Brian wondered why his father suddenly pretended to care about how he talked, how he dressed, how he wore his hair, what music he listened to, and what friends he chose. From Brian's perspective, it was a little late to get involved, especially if involvement equaled criticism. He pretended to listen to his father to avoid additional consequences, but internally he negated every command.

"I don't know how many times I have to tell you this, but you won't use that language in my house." (Your *house? You're never here. Besides, what about* your *language?)*

"Brian, listen to me, you keep dressing like that and doing your hair that way, people are going to think you're something you're not." *(You know what I am? That's funny.)*

"Turn that music off. I don't want you listening to whatever that is." *(I would love to see you try to stop me.)*

"Son, I don't want that Chris kid coming over here anymore. He's a bad influence on you. I don't know why you run around with such trash." *(So now I'm your son. By the way, Chris cares more about me than you ever will. I guess that's why you think he's trash.)*

Now that Brian was in high school, things were even worse. In an attempt to control him, Bruce added a punishment to the end of every lecture. Brian showed no signs of improvement, so Bruce

 FAITH UNPLUGGED:

Your parents need God and his forgiveness just as you do.

concluded that he needed additional motivation to change his ways. Bruce's disciplinary attempts infuriated his son. Brian no longer restrained his tongue. After all, Bruce wasn't home enough to enforce his punishments, so why pretend to listen or obey? Quickly, the lectures turned into intense arguments. Today was one of those days, and the argument in the car felt like the last straw to Brian.

Later, after Brian had finished with his stocking, he came to ask his uncle what needed to be done next. Uncle Ron showed him a fertilizer spreader that needed to be assembled as a floor model. He handed Brian the toolbox, and then asked, "So what happened this time? With Bruce, I mean. And why do you call him 'Bruce' and not 'dad'?"

Brian said, "Oh, I started calling him 'Bruce' because he doesn't seem like a 'dad' to me. Not like my friends' dads. Anyway, my grades came in the mail today. Bruce wasn't pleased to see a B next to Algebra II. In fact, he said the grade was completely unacceptable. 'There's no reasonable explanation for this poor performance,'" Brian said, mimicking his father's tone and actions.

"He said that about a B in Algebra II?"

"I know! Can you believe it? He makes me so angry, pretending to be the interested father. I'm sick of his little lectures, and I'm sick of how he feels good afterwards, like he's some kind of model dad. I know he's your brother, but I can't stand him. Two more years of this hell, and after that I'm leaving and never coming back."

"What about your mom?"

"She can visit me if she wants."

"Would you mind if I shared something with you, Brian?" Uncle Ron asked.

"Sure," Brian responded hesitantly.

"Not having kids myself, I don't know what kind of dad I'd make, but to me it sounds as if Bruce acts just like our dad did."

"Grandpa?" Brian asked, shocked.

"Your grandpa has changed quite a bit over the years, but when we were younger, things were rough between us. Things were so bad, I actually left home early to get away from him. So did your dad. Neither one of us could care less what happened to him or if we ever saw him again. I hated him and made sure he knew it."

"Are you serious?" Brian inquired again, still shocked at what he was hearing.

"We didn't talk for years after I left. I don't know if your dad talks with him much even now."

"That sounds good to me right about now," Brian muttered.

"Actually, I was miserable. Living with hatred toward a parent sours life."

"So what happened?" Brian asked.

"Well, when I became a Christian, I knew I was supposed to honor my father. I figured I was exempt because Dad was a jerk, but it kept bothering me. I spent a couple of years wrestling with the idea of honoring someone I hated. During that time, I learned to do two things that really helped. One was to ask the questions: Why was my dad the way he was? Why was he so angry? Why did he work so much? Why did he drink all the time? Why was he emotionally disconnected? Asking the questions and looking for the answers helped me see my dad as a real person. I think *his* dad treated him badly too ... and I wanted to break that cycle."

"I never thought about that before," Brian said.

"The second thing I learned was to be grateful, and I started praying for him. Every day. I realized that my dad played a big role in giving me life. Then it moved onto other things. My dad actually taught me a lot. For example, Dad valued doing your best. I learned the importance of doing the same. My perspective and my expectations slowly changed, as did our relationship. Don't get me wrong. It wasn't quick or easy, but it was worth it. Honestly, it would have been worth it even if he never changed. I needed to go through that process; otherwise, I think I would have made the same mistakes he did. Anyway, I thought it might give you a little different perspective. Hope that helps a little."

"Yeah," Brian said with a smile. "I think it does."

 ## FAITH LINK:

Jesus, show me how to honor my father and my mother, especially when they hurt, frustrate, or annoy me. Give me eyes to see them the way you see them. Give me a heart to love, forgive, obey, and pray for them even when I don't want to.

 ## POWER UP:

What is the first thing that comes to mind when you think of your mom? What about your dad? Are the things that come to your mind positive or negative? If they are positive, have you thanked them lately? If they're negative, have you forgiven them and prayed for them lately? If you have a good relationship with your parents, be careful not to take them for granted. Spend time with them and express your gratitude. If you have a hard relationship with one or both of your parents, today would be a great day to begin working on that relationship. Ask God to heal your hurts and change your heart toward your mom or dad.

NOT THE ONLY ONE

Anger with God

DOWNLOAD:

For [God] has not despised or disdained the suffering of the afflicted one; he has not hidden his face from him but has listened to his cry for help. Psalm 22:24 NIV

Alan sat motionless in the back of the room. His glazed eyes fixated on the floor. People shuffled around, whispering to one another between hugs and handshakes. A few people glanced in Alan's direction, quiet murmurs of pity wafting over to him. He prayed they would leave without talking to him, but he knew better. *Apparently,* he thought, *God doesn't answer prayer—at least not mine.*

Alan's father, James, stood at the front of the church surrounded by family, friends, and flowers. His eyes looked tired, but grateful, as he gently smiled and greeted the next person in line. "Thank you for coming, Ann. We appreciate your prayers and support."

"I'm so sorry, James. Please let me know if there's anything I can do for you and the kids." Trying to hold back her tears, Ann looked into the casket to see her friend one last time. "She looks so peaceful."

"Yes, she does. I'm glad she's no longer suffering," James answered. His voice broke as he looked down at his wife of twenty years, the mother of his three children, and his best friend. A single tear rolled down the side of his face; there were not many tears left. The last year and a half had taken its toll.

As the receiving line continued in front of his father, images and questions flooded Alan's mind. He saw his mom smiling proudly as he stood onstage during his first high school vocal concert. He pictured her laughing as she read the birthday card he gave her two years ago. He remembered her listening to his worries about crushes who didn't seem to like him back. Mostly, he remembered her bald head lying in a bed connected to an incessant number of machines as she attempted to make light of her own burdens by asking him about his.

Why did she have to die? Why her? Why not someone who deserved it? She was a good person. Why would you do this to her, God? What did she ever do to you? Why, God? What did any of us do to deserve this?

Eventually the questions in his mind became conversation in his heart. *I don't understand you. You claim to be a God of love, yet you let people who love you get sick and die. You are supposed to be all powerful, yet you do nothing. You tell us to pray and ask for your help, but you don't answer. It's like you get some sick pleasure out of us asking you, knowing all along that you're not going to respond. As far as I'm concerned, you no longer exist. I don't even know why I'm bothering to talk to you.*

As the weeks went by following the funeral, Alan thought perhaps the dull pain of loss might lessen, but his disappointment turned into rage. The church had a gym, and Alan found that he could pound out his frustration on the punching bag. He was stopping by every day after school now, running laps and then pounding the punching bag until he felt the anger and hurt melt away from sheer tiredness.

One day as he stood panting following his laps, he noticed Todd Beckwith doing crunches on a machine across the gym. Todd was on staff with Young Life and frequented Alan's school on a regular basis. Alan liked Todd, but since his mom died, Alan had avoided him and everyone else he thought might give him some clichéd answer about why his mom died and how God was in control. But today, something compelled him to go talk with Todd.

"Can I work in on this machine?" Alan asked.

"Sure, Alan. How you been, man?"

What kind of question is that? How do you think I am? Did you not see the casket when you walked in? You idiot. Alan managed to stop his tongue from repeating the words in his head and instead answered, "I'm fine. Just doing my workout. What are you doing here?"

"The church has been letting me work out here, which is great. Hey, I'm really sorry about your mom." Todd got up from the machine and wiped it down so Alan could use it. "I think I know how you feel."

Again, Alan halted his tongue and whispered a sarcastic, "Yeah, right."

"I was sixteen," Todd said quietly. He had picked up a pair of dumbbells and begun doing some curls as Alan did his crunches.

FAITH UNPLUGGED:

Our emotions don't threaten God. Instead, he invites us to bring them to him, even if he is their target.

"What?" The statement grabbed Alan's attention. He paused, midcrunch.

"I was sixteen when my dad died in a car accident. A drunk driver hit him coming home from one of my away games. I remember sitting at his funeral feeling so angry. I was angry with the driver, who survived the accident, but I was furious with God. I just didn't get it. Nothing added up for me at that point. All my life, my parents talked about God in these positive, feel-good terms. It was easy to believe because life was easy. When he died, my entire belief system died with him."

"What do you mean?" Alan already knew the answer, but he wanted to hear someone else say it so he didn't feel so alone.

"I began to question everything I ever heard about God being a good God. If he was so good, then why did my dad die and the drunk live? If God was so good, why did my mom have to go through so much pain? Why did I have to lose my dad? I had a million questions and no answers. If God let my dad die, why should I care about him or what he has to say? I figured that God turned his back on me, and I returned the favor. I walked away from everything remotely connected to God. I buried my faith with my dad."

Alan vacated the machine and sat down next to Todd. For the first time since his mom's diagnosis, Alan felt like someone understood, but it confused him to hear this from Todd. "But you obviously got over it, right?"

"Well, no. Not really. I mean, I still miss my dad. But I did get my faith back. I was a good kid until my dad died, then my life kind of spun out of control. When I walked away from God, I just stopped caring, or I pretended not to care. I really wanted to get even with God. I thought I would pay him back by doing everything I knew was wrong. The problem was that it didn't work; things only got worse for me. I lost my friends, quit playing sports, and almost dropped out of school. Worst of all, I couldn't shake the idea of God. As much as I wanted to live as if he was dead or turn my back on him, I couldn't.

"And I know God never let me go, even when I thought I hated him. Eventually, I knew that I was hurting myself by my actions, and that God still was a force in my life whether I wanted him to be or not. So I figured I had only one course of action."

"What was that?"

"Forgiveness. If I was going to live like God didn't exist, then I couldn't hold him responsible for my dad's death. The process of forgiveness caused me to reconsider everything that happened. In turn, it forced me to reconsider God. Slowly, I began to embrace the possibility that horrible things can happen in life and God can still be good. It might seem illogical, but accepting the possibility ignited my journey back to God."

Todd paused briefly, put his hand on Alan's shoulder, and continued, "Anyway, I just wanted you to know that you're not the only one. If you want to talk more, give me a call sometime."

Alan looked at Todd's number, stuffed it in his pocket as he stood, and walked toward the punching bag for one more round.

FAITH LINK:

God, I'm angry, and the person I'm angry with is you. I don't understand why life is so difficult or why you seem to do nothing about it. Honestly, I feel like Jesus on the cross, as if you've turned your back on me. Yet, I know there is more going on than I can understand. Help me to understand what I can. Help me to trust you.

POWER UP:

Have you ever been angry or disappointed with God? How about frustrated or annoyed? What about hurt or confused? You're not the only one. There are others around you who have felt the same way. The Bible, especially the Old Testament books like Psalms, Job, and Lamentations, contains many stories of God's people throughout history who experienced the same emotions. Through Jesus, God became man. He understands the human dilemma. Your emotions don't turn him away from you, but they might turn you away from him if you allow them. Talk to him about how you feel. Express your feelings, then give him time to respond.

A TOUGH BREAK

Disappointment

DOWNLOAD:

Unrelenting disappointment leaves you heartsick, but a sudden good break can turn life around. Proverbs 13:12

Zach Collins stood at the end of aisle five holding a scrap piece of paper and looking confused. "Hey, Collins! Are you ready or what?" Tyler Ham hollered down the aisle of the grocery store. Startled, Zach looked up to see his teammate and fellow senior strolling toward him.

"What's up, Ham? How's your summer been?" Zach inquired, as the two football players shook hands.

"Who cares? The important thing is that camp is two weeks away. This is our year, man! Are you pumped or what?"

"Oh yeah. I can't wait to get the season rolling," Zach responded casually.

"You didn't see the sports page this morning, did you?" Tyler asked, annoyed by his friend's lack of excitement.

"No. What did it say?"

"For starters, they put your ugly face on the first page under the caption: 'Collins poised to lead the Cardinals all the way!' Of course, they mentioned me in the article as well."

"There was a whole article?"

"You know it. The preseason rankings came out. We're number one!"

"Seriously? Sweet!" Zach replied, slightly more excited.

"Yes, it is. It's going to be a good year. I can feel it. Anyway, I gotta run. Mom sent me for some milk. See ya soon, Collins." Ham's voice faded as he bounced down the aisle toward the dairy case.

Zach finished gathering the items on the grocery list and headed for checkout. Noticing a stack of newspapers, he grabbed one. *Mom's going to want to read this,* he justified while imagining the size of his picture.

His mom was standing in the kitchen as he hurried through the door. He tossed the grocery sacks on the counter and scurried past his dad, who was sitting at the table enjoying his morning coffee. Zach jumped on the chair, opening the paper like a four-year-old with a present at Christmas.

"Good morning, Son."

"Oh. Morning, Dad," Zach responded without breaking his concentration.

"What has you so excited about reading this morning?"

"The preseason football rankings were released today. We're number one! My picture is in the paper and everything. Listen to this: 'With seven returning starters including preseason all-state quarterback Zach Collins, the Cardinals will run away with the North Central Conference on their way to their first state championship in school history.'"

"Zach, that's great. I'm so proud of you. Congratulations!"

"Thanks, Dad."

The weeks leading up to camp ticked away. The team was the talk of the town as everyone anxiously awaited the start of the season. Zach, Tyler, and the rest of the team had become celebrities, and they were enjoying the attention. Camp, which was really an excuse to start two-a-day practices a week early, started with a buzz of excitement, a hint of arrogance, and a determination to win at all costs.

Coach Jefferson scripted his pep talks to the delight of the invading press. By week's end, the summer rust had worn off, and the team appeared primed for full-contact practices.

The weeks continued to race by as school began and the Cardinals' annual "Red and Black" scrimmage neared. The beginning of classes fed Cardinal fever. The students, teachers, and administrators talked nonstop about the team as if they themselves would be on the field. "We're unstoppable!" The cheerleaders and pep squad littered the hallways with posters. "Watch out, state. The Cardinals are coming!" The marching band added an early-morning practice to prepare for the big crowds. Even the lunch ladies became zealous, adding red and black food coloring to everything imaginable.

By Friday night's scrimmage, the excitement had turned to mass hysteria. The "Red and Black" scrimmage surprisingly felt like the play-offs. Everyone was excited, especially the players. They could not wait to show off their talent, particularly those who were still fighting for a starting spot.

The opening kickoff set the tone for the game. The Black Team huddled on the twenty-two yard line around its captain. Zach barked out the first play, "Four ten Z-Right Slant on Two. Ready ..."

"Break" the offense yelled as they hustled to the line.

"Hut! Hut!" yelled Zach, and the center snapped the ball. Zach stepped back three steps and saw his receiver, Brian Rodriguez, break loose in the middle of the field. The quarterback slung a beautiful spiral over the middle linebacker's head and into Brian's outstretched hands. Brian caught the pass in perfect stride, allowing him to speed past the Red Team's cornerback and safety for a long touchdown. The crowd went crazy! This was exactly what they expected to see all year long.

As the game continued, the Cardinals continued to impress as the Red and Black entered into a seesaw battle. Nearing the end of the second quarter, Black was leading by a score of 21-14 with the ball on the Red forty-two yard line after a fumble recovery. Zach marched his offense back on the field and confidently called another play, "Six twenty Trips Left Fade on One. Ready ..."

Like a well-oiled machine, the offense yelled, "Break," clapped their hands, and rushed to their positions. Zach surveyed the defense before lining up under center. "Hut!" he bellowed as he dropped into the pocket. *One more second,* he thought as he pre-pared to launch another pass. *Now!* He unleashed another spectacular pass just before being nailed by the oncoming defensive lineman. The pass floated over the shoulder of his receiver as he crossed into the end zone, landing flawlessly into his hands. TOUCHDOWN! The crowd erupted again, jumping and screaming as if this were the greatest play they had ever witnessed.

The cheering stopped abruptly as the coach and trainer ran onto the field. A Black player was down and obviously in pain. "Who is it?" everyone asked, trying to glimpse the player's number.

Zach was lying on the field cradling his right arm—screaming.

A few hours later a crowd gathered around outside of the emergency room at the local hospital. Black won the game, but no one cared. The town waited silently.

FAITH UNPLUGGED:

No disappointment lies beyond God's ability to redeem it or walk you through it.

In the emergency room Zach sat with his father as the doctor finished applying the cast. "That ought to do it."

Zach looked at his dad. His dad looked back. They were thinking the same thing—*Who's going to ask?*

"So, how long, Doc?" Mr. Collins asked hesitantly, fearing the worse.

"I'm afraid you're not going to like what I have to say. Zach, your arm is fractured in two places and your hand in three. They were clean breaks, so if all goes well you won't need surgery. We won't know for sure for a month. Either way, I would say six months minimum."

Zach's face fell. His eyes welled up despite his efforts to blink the tears back.

Zach and his dad turned and left the emergency room. "Zach, I'm so sorry. I don't know what to say. You must be so disappointed."

"Disappointed? Dad, I'm *devastated*! I can't believe this is happening to me. It wasn't supposed to be like this."

"I know, Son, but I promise you it's going to be OK. We're going to get through this ... together. Now why don't you take a few minutes to yourself? There's quite a crowd out there waiting for an update. I'll go fill them in. When you're ready, come on out."

A few minutes passed. Zach slowly pulled his jacket over one arm and slung the other side over his shoulder. He made the long walk down the cold corridor toward the waiting room. He passed through the doors and walked into a lobby full of his friends, family, teammates, teachers, and coaches. The moment they saw Zach, they cheered and burst into applause. Slowly, a smile worked its way across Zach's face.

FAITH LINK:

Jesus, life is not meeting my expectations. When I think things are going one way, they go another instead. This constant disappointment is crushing me. I need a good break or a change of perspective. I want things to go my way, but even more, I want my life to go your way. If my plans or expectations need an adjustment, change me.

POWER UP:

Think about the times in your life when you've been disappointed. How did you respond? What happened in the time that followed? Did God bring something good into your life around the same time? Did he create something beautiful out of the disappointment itself? What did he teach you? Now think about the times in your life when you were not disappointed or even the times that exceeded your expectations. Ask yourself the same questions. In your life, you will experience excellent opportunities as well as tough breaks. How you respond matters. God will use both of them to direct your life or to show his love. God is always working in your life. Encourage yourself by considering what he has done in the past or what he promises to do in the future.

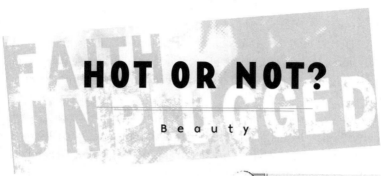

HOT OR NOT?

Beauty

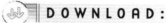

DOWNLOAD:

Charm can mislead and beauty soon fades. The woman to be admired and praised is the woman who lives in the Fear-of-GOD.
Proverbs 31:30

It had all begun four days ago. Monday morning, February 27 to be exact. Before the first bell rang, the word began to spread. Misty Buford, a junior, entered the commons with an assured look and a knowing smile. She walked briskly to her table. As soon as her friends saw her, they knew what was up, but they waited. Misty leaned on the table, and spoke only a few words: "Prom is now in session."

Daniel was good looking, single, smart, talented, popular, kind, and humble. As such, everyone was wondering about his prom choice. Like most people, he loved the attention. And he enjoyed the drama (at least to a point). However, he was rapidly nearing the point where it was driving him nuts. Daniel had several appealing options, but kept coming back around to one girl.

Once he'd made up his mind, the question of the day—"Who are you going to take to prom?"—went from entertaining to annoying. It wasn't lighthearted anymore. He was starting to feel the pressure.

During sixth hour, the pressure built to an uncontrollable level because of Misty. Misty served as the school's self-appointed social chair. Her primary responsibility—knowing everyone's social agenda. Prom for a social chair resembles April for accountants. By

Friday, Daniel had become her primary target. Misty knew Mrs. Kirby's vocal class would be the best time to talk because "we never do anything in vocal class." So she arrived early and waited by the door.

Daniel walked to class with Blake, Mary, and his twin sister, Bethany. Blake Owens, Daniel's best friend, had inoculated himself from the prom drama when he began dating Amber in December. Bethany planned to go with a bunch of her friends. As they approached the door, Daniel and Blake paused to let Mary and Bethany enter class first.

When Daniel walked through the door, Misty grabbed him by the arm and dragged him to an empty seat. Blake, Mary, and Bethany rolled their eyes, chuckled, and followed.

"Daniel, you know what today is, right?"

"Yeah, Misty. It's Friday."

"Wrong answer. It's exactly fifty-six days until prom, and as far as I know, you don't have a date," Misty retorted.

"Really? Fifty-six days. That's all?" Daniel joked.

"Not funny," Misty continued, unfazed by the wisecrack. "The way I figure it, you have six high-profile options. First, there's Summer Daniels. She is absolutely gorgeous and way fun. She's turned down a couple of guys already. I think she's totally waiting for you to ask.

"Option two: Rachel McMurray, who happens to be one of my best friends. I can guarantee she will say yes because I just talked to her last hour. Just between you and me, though, Ryan Franks might ask her too. She'll say yes to whoever asks first.

"Third on the list would be the lovely and talented Miss Naomi Granger." Misty seemed to be deriving real pleasure from her presentation. "As you know, Naomi has been offered three full-ride basketball scholarships to Division-One schools."

"Dude, she's like four inches taller than you are!" Blake interjected.

"Pipe down, Owens! This is my show," Misty snapped. She really was enjoying herself. "Fourth, moving down to the juniors, we find Rebekah Thomas. Yes, she might be a little socially awkward, but imagine showing your prom pictures to your college roommate. She is by far the most beautiful girl in the school. You would look amazing together."

"She's right, Daniel. Rebekah really is beautiful," Mary chimed in with a sly smile.

"On to number five."

"Did you really make a list?" Bethany asked in disbelief, and everyone laughed.

"As I was saying, in the five spot, we have Ramona Evans. Unfortunate name but great legs. Plus, you have seventh hour together so it would be easy for you to connect to coordinate colors."

FAITH UNPLUGGED:

The things that make people truly beautiful lie beneath the surface.

"It's, like, so important to coordinate your colors," Mary said with a twinkle in her eye.

"Last but not least, the woman with the most contagious smile this high school has ever seen, Kellie Kaufmann. She's the cutest. So, which one is it going to be, Daniel?"

"Well ... maybe Misty doesn't know as much as she thinks she does." Daniel smiled and shrugged.

"Maybe you should just take them all," whispered Mrs. Kirby conspiratorially as she walked by. Everyone burst out laughing as she winked and flashed a thumbs-up.

"Whatever. Actually, I've already asked someone."

"Who?" everyone cried in unison.

"I think I know," said Bethany.

Daniel refused to say another word. But later in the hallway, Bethany cornered him. "Well ...?" she demanded.

Daniel smiled. "Who do you think it is?"

"Is it Mary?"

"You guessed it, Sis. How'd you know?"

"Well, I knew none of Misty's selections were your type. And then I saw you glance at Mary a couple of times."

"Good eye. I always have so much fun with Mary. Plus, I wanted to share prom with someone I really care about and not just pick someone based on popularity or how she looks."

"I'm impressed. Mary has more inner beauty than all those other girls combined. And she has great legs!" she said with a wink.

FAITH LINK:

Jesus, I want to be the kind of person who values the right things. Too many times I focus on the physical appearance of others and myself. I make it the most important thing when it's not. You created everyone in your image. Help me to see that everyone is beautiful, and help me to place more value on people's character and heart, including my own.

POWER UP:

We live in a culture that assigns people a value based on their appearance. People rate and rank each other's "hotness" on TV, the Internet, and in conversations. Those who score high enjoy privileges and treatment denied to the rest of us. You have probably done the same thing or had someone do it to you. There are all sorts of problems with this system. It reduces the people God created in his image to a number or an object. It separates, isolates, and hurts people. And it places emphasis on something few people can control and that will change drastically with age. In this system, someone can be popular, powerful, or influential and not be good or kind. Resist the temptation to do this to others or to yourself. Treat everyone with dignity, honor, and respect. Furthermore, strive to recognize and champion the things that God deems beautiful.

NO BIG DEAL

Cheating

🎧 **DOWNLOAD:**

God hates cheating in the marketplace; he loves it when business is aboveboard. Proverbs 11:1

Alex stumbled out of the classroom in a daze. "What was *that?*" he asked no one in particular. "This class is going to be the death of me."

Alex had started school expecting to coast through his senior year. Instead, a new nemesis had arrived on the scene, quickly shattering Alex's illusions. His name, Mr. Robertson. His class, senior government. Mr. Robertson was an ex-Navy Seal turned university professor tired of dealing with undisciplined and unprepared college students. He had quit his high-profile, well-paid university position and moved to a small Midwestern town to "adequately prepare high school students for academia."

Robertson accomplished his mission through a simple but effective method. He taught the state-required senior government class exactly as he did at the university. On the first day of class, he handed out a syllabus outlining every lecture, assignment, paper, and exam including minimum requirements and due dates. After reviewing the contents to ensure that every student understood his expectations, he informed the class, "From this moment on, you have no reason to ask me any questions about the required workload and no excuse for missing any assignments.

Finally, I want to remind you that you must pass this class in order to graduate. Thank you. You are dismissed."

Students filed out of the class in shocked silence. No story or warning could match the dread of the actual experience. Unfortunately, most students misunderstood Mr. Robertson. He genuinely cared. He really wanted them to succeed. He was a phenomenal teacher with a brilliant plan. However, most considered him the Devil's third cousin. This year was no different.

The stress reduced the Washington High seniors to the most primeval forms of communication ... tears, grunts, moans, and groans. Eventually, their language skills returned: "You've got to be kidding me!" "He can't be serious." "This is officially the worst day of my life." "If I fail, I won't graduate. If I don't graduate, I won't be able to go to college."

Later that evening, the students resigned themselves to the tasks before them. Whining and worrying wouldn't help them read the introduction and first chapter of their dictionary-thick American Government book. Nor would it help them answer the discussion questions at the end of the chapter. Nor would it prepare them for the vocabulary quiz set to occur on Thursday. They had no choice but to do the work.

By the end of the first week, many of the seniors had developed deep bags under their eyes. A few seemed to be slowly adjusting to the new rhythm. Their classmates' responses ranged from frustrated avoidance to jealous name-calling to humble pleas for help.

Monday morning arrived too quickly as the seniors gathered in the commons retelling their weekend adventures in study. The conversation inevitably turned to the government assignment due today. "So did everyone finish reading chapter three?" Sunny asked.

"Yeah," Alex replied. "I started reading it last night about ten. I almost forgot about it until Jeff IMed me with a reminder. I've never read so much in one sitting! My eyes were bugging out. I could barely stay awake. Reading about Jefferson Democrats wasn't exactly helping my cause."

Justin laughed. "You mean Jeffersonian Democracy."

"Whatever!" Alex quipped. Everyone laughed.

"And did everyone finish reading last week's *Newsweek?*" Sunny asked.

"*Newsweek?* What are you talking about?" Alex's voice jumped an octave as the question startled him into an elevated threat level.

"Don't you remember on the first day Mr. Robertson told us to pick up a copy of *Newsweek*, read it, and answer the questions provided in the syllabus?" Sunny began to sound like Mr. Robertson as she continued, "He encouraged us to order a subscription because this was going to be a weekly assignment. He wants us to be up-to-date on our national and world affairs."

 FAITH UNPLUGGED:

You can justify or rationalize anything, but it will not change reality or the consequences.

"Hmm. Let me think ... NO! Of course I didn't remember. If I had remembered, why would I have asked?" Alex was irate and blood rushed to his face. Calming himself slightly, he asked, "What am I going to do?"

"Dude, don't stress about it. Here, take my answers. You've got English first hour, right?" Justin asked.

"Yeah"

"Copy down my answers, change a few words here and there, and then give it back to me between classes."

"You serious?"

"You bet!"

"Thanks, Justin. I owe you."

"How about you spot me next week? You read the *Newsweek* article, answer the questions, and I'll get them from you. If it works out, we can keep rotating weeks. It will make government a whole lot easier," Justin said with a smug glint in his eye.

Sunny tried to stay quiet, but the words slipped out: "Isn't that, like, cheating?"

"Cheating? Are you kidding me? No way," Justin defended. "Sunny, it's no big deal. It's *Newsweek,* not a test. Right? It's not like we're breaking into Robertson's office, stealing the answer key, mass-producing it, and selling the copies on eBay for a nice profit."

"But that's not a bad idea!" Alex joked to keep the atmosphere loose. "Seriously, though, this is no different than if we sat down and did the homework together. It's like when you and I help each other with our math homework during lunch. Besides, I talked to my older brother; everyone does this kind of stuff to pass government. Like Justin said, it's no big deal." Even as he said it, a twinge of guilt flashed through his gut.

The first bell rang, ending the conversation. Alex grabbed Justin's paper and chuckled as he headed to his AP English class. As soon as he sat down, he began frantically transcribing, finding pleasure in artfully modifying Justin's prose. By the time Miss Anderson finished taking attendance, he was nearly finished. He could sense the impending relief. *Just a few more questions to go—*

"Mr. Horner?

"Mr. Horner.

"Mr. *Horner!*"

"Yes, ma'am!" Alex choked as he realized what was happening. Miss Anderson marched toward his desk. Trying to maintain eye contact, Alex attempted to slide Justin's paper under his own without drawing attention to it.

"Can I ask what you're doing that is so important?"

Regaining his composure, Alex said, "I'm sorry, Miss Anderson. I was trying to finish my government assignment. It won't happen again."

"Government, eh? What kind of torture is Mr. Robertson currently administering?" Miss Anderson solicited as she reached down to examine his paper. Instantly, she realized what was happening and grabbed both papers. "Oh, that's right. Monday is *Newsweek* day. You seem to have some very interesting reflections on last week's articles. How about I hold onto these and we can talk about your insights after class?"

The class fell silent. Miss Anderson walked the papers to her desk. A thousand scenarios rushed through Alex's mind. He sank down in his chair and lowered his head. Suddenly, "borrowing" Justin's answers seemed like a bigger deal. He was certain Justin's beliefs were about to change as well.

FAITH LINK:

Jesus, sometimes I can justify things so quickly and easily in my mind. I can turn big things into small things with a few words. Eventually, I know I'll realize how big they really are. I want to realize it now. If there are things in my life that I'm minimizing, reveal them to me. Help me to stop now instead of later.

POWER UP:

Cheating has become a national pastime. Professional athletes cheat with performance-enhancing drugs. People cheat on their taxes. Husbands and wives cheat on each other. Students cheat on quizzes, tests, and homework. Studies say cheating is becoming more common and more acceptable in society. Calling cheating "borrowing" doesn't change what it is any more than calling a lie an "exaggeration" changes it. The human mind is not the standard of right and wrong. God is. Think about your life. Are you living according to your standard or God's? Why? If your answer is because it's quicker or easier, then you value speed and efficiency more than you value doing the right thing. Do you want to live your life that way? How will that affect your future? Think about your education, your job, your marriage, and your future. What is more important—the quick and easy or the right and good?

THIS, THAT, OR THE OTHER?

Priorities   and   Choices

DOWNLOAD:

Who, then, is the man that fears the LORD? He will instruct him in the way chosen for him. Psalm 25:12 NIV

The anticipation of summer didn't excite sixteen-year-old Reggie, a sophomore. He needed a job to pay off the car he bought shortly after his birthday. His parents lent him the money with the understanding that he would work this summer.

On the other hand, Garrett, Reggie's best friend and football teammate, could not wait for summer to start. He needed a break after a stressful year of balancing student council, football, basketball, track, band, school, church, and his prolific social agenda.

José, the group's lone junior, felt the pressure of choosing a college, which he planned to spend his summer researching. Summer excited him because he wanted to get the monkey of indecision off his back. If one more person asked him, "What are you going to do after you graduate next year?" he would go crazy. "Other than Cedric Duff, I don't know anyone who knows what they're doing after next year," José wailed. "But then, Cedric knew in fourth grade. Wish I did. Why can't I just decide?"

Ignoring their friend's incessant ranting, Reggie and Garrett went on with their conversation. College was another year off for them, and they had more pressing concerns. "What are you thinking about for a job right now?" Garrett asked Reggie. "Have you even applied anywhere yet?"

"Um, not really. I can't decide what I want to do. I could try to get a job at Electronics Unlimited for the discounts, but I'm afraid I'd spend all my money instead of paying my parents back. There are the ice-cream shops and the fast-food scene. My dad offered me a job at his company filing papers, which sounds pretty boring, but the pay is good. Then my mom told me about this summer-camp counselor thing, which sounds really cool, but then I'd be out of town all summer."

"Well, then that's definitely not an option. If I have the whole summer free and you're gone, what am I supposed to do with my time? It's just not an option," said Garrett.

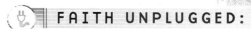

FAITH UNPLUGGED:

What we really value displays itself in the choices we make.

"Maybe I should spend a year or two at Edgewood Community College and then figure this out later," José continued, oblivious that no one was listening.

"Yeah, I know it would really stink to be gone all summer." A debate was forming in Reggie's mind. "But I think it would be fun to work with kids all summer."

"No way, Reggie. I can't let you do it. I think you should either take the job with your dad for the money or at a restaurant, so I can eat free all summer long."

"I wonder," José kept going, "if they're just trying to make conversation. Maybe they don't expect an answer. They could just be talking to fill the silence. On the other hand, they could feel obligated. Hmmm?" Pausing briefly, he asked his friends, "What do you think?" They looked at him blankly.

José threw in the towel and joined in the dispute. "I actually think the summer-camp idea sounds fun." Apparently he'd been listening to them.

"You do?" Reggie inquired. "I thought so too."

"Who asked you?" Garrett joked.

"Definitely," José said. "I don't want you to be gone all summer either, but it's a great opportunity. You get to spend the entire summer hanging out with a bunch of cool kids. Think about the difference that would make in their lives. Plus you get paid and won't be tempted to spend any money going to the movies with us. It's a win-win."

"But think about all the things you'll miss," countered Garrett. "Hanging out with us. Going to the lake. Cookouts. Late-night drives. Sleeping in." Running low on ideas, he repeated, "Hanging out with us ..."

"But I have to get a job," Reggie reminded him.

"There will still be plenty of time leftover for a job," Garrett said.

"I know staying here would be a blast, but I think José's right. Spending my time this summer with those kids could make a lot of difference in their lives and probably mine, too. I think I'm going to look into it some more."

"Suit yourself," Garrett huffed as they walked off to their next classes.

A few days, a few phone calls, and a few prayers later, Reggie made up his mind. For some reason, he felt that working at the camp was what God wanted him to do. "Summer camp, here I come!"

Only two things left to do. Tell the guys and tell his football coach, which should be easier than telling Garrett. He decided to talk to Coach Gregory first.

"Well, that sounds like a great opportunity for you." Coach Gregory began his response after Reggie stuttered through his announcement. "But I have to say, I'm a little disappointed, and I'm sure the team will be too. Since you won't be here this summer, you won't be participating in the summer workout program. And I have to keep that in mind when I put together the roster in the fall. You could be sacrificing your place on this team. Are you sure you want to do that?"

Coach Gregory caught Reggie off guard. He hadn't considered that option. He thought Coach would be cool with his decision. His mind was racing, and Coach could see it. "It looks like you have more to think about than you thought. Take a day or two and get back to me." Coach patted his shoulder and walked away.

"I told you staying here was the best decision," Garrett responded after Reggie had recapped his interaction with their coach. "I didn't even think about using football in my argument. That settles it then ... right?"

His confidence turned to question as he noticed Reggie's response.

"I don't know. I have a lot to consider. Don't get me wrong. I do want to play in the fall, but I feel like this summer-camp thing is what I'm supposed to be doing right now. I need to figure out if it's worth potentially sacrificing football."

FAITH LINK:

Jesus, there are so many ways that I could spend my time, and so many people and things fighting for my time. I know I can't do everything or please everyone. Show me what you want me to do and how to please you.

POWER UP:

Do you ever have trouble making decisions or choosing your priorities? You know that you can't do everything, so you have to choose. Choosing how to spend the little time you have is hard, and it's extremely important. How you spend your time, or how you spend your money, reveals what you care about most. Many people value the opinions of others, so they do what they think those people want them to do. They base their priorities on the acceptance of others. Others put money, sports, education, or relationships first. What comes first in your life?

How does that influence your decision making? Have you considered what God might want you to do? Have you thought about focusing on that and trusting him with everything else? Try it! It's the best way to live.

MY BIGGEST PET PEEVE

Role Models

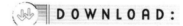

DOWNLOAD:

Don't let anyone put you down because you're young. Teach believers with your life: by word, by demeanor, by love, by faith, by integrity. 1 Timothy 4:12

"All right, everyone now understands pronoun-antecedent agreement, right?" asked Mrs. Thomas.

"Absolutely!" answered Vince Gibson, the class clown, causing a ripple of laughter. He was speaking in a Donald Duck voice again.

"Thank you for that, Mr. Gibson." Mrs. Thomas smiled as she walked back to her desk. "We have just enough time remaining to discuss your next paper. Before I give you the assignment, let me just say that I expect improvement in your writing—specifically in the areas we talked about in class or that I addressed on your last paper. Is that understood?"

"Absolutely!" Vince quacked again. His second attempt generated a bigger response from both the students and the teacher.

"Mr. Gibson! Are you finished?" Her voice was stern, but her eyes twinkled.

"Absolutely!" Vince said in the duck voice, grinning ear to ear.

"Thank you, *Donald,*" Mrs. Thomas quipped, shooting him a look of bemused warning. "Now, class, your next paper will be due one week from today."

"One week?" A groan arose from the students.

Mrs. Thomas didn't pause or acknowledge the complaint. "The subject of the paper will be your biggest pet peeve. If you don't know what a pet peeve is, use Mr. Gibson as your example," she said with a sly smile.

"That was low, Mrs. T. Low." Vince slid lower in his chair. The duck voice was gone, but his smile was still present.

"I want the paper to be three pages in length, single-spaced, twelve-point Times New Roman type with one-inch margins on all four sides. Is that clear?" She peered at Billy Sands, who had attempted to use inch-and-a-quarter margins on his last paper. "If there are no further questions, you're dismissed."

Dan Morris and Vince exited class together on their way to lunch. "What's your biggest pet peeve, Morris?"

"Other than you?"

"Ha, ha. Seriously though, what is it?"

"This is going to be the easiest paper I've ever written. The moment she said 'pet peeve,' I saw a huge picture of my little brother's face right in front of my eyes." Dan wriggled his fingers in front of his face.

"You're going to write about little Morris? Man, I like that kid."

"You don't live with him."

"Thank God. Then I would be living with you, too."

"Shut up," Dan said with a lighthearted shove.

Later that night, Dan started working on his paper. Normally he procrastinated until the night before an assignment was due. Today, however, all he could think about was the assignment. He kept remembering story after story that perfectly illustrated what annoyed him about his younger brother. Dan seized the opportunity to translate his thoughts onto paper before he forgot.

Surprised by his older brother's sudden interest in homework, David walked into Dan's room without knocking of course. "Hey, Dan, what are you doing?" he asked, peering over his brother's shoulder.

"What's it look like I'm doing?" It only took three seconds for the irritation to take effect.

"Writing, duh! I'm not stupid. Whatcha writing about?"

"I'll give you one guess."

Immediately, David's eight-year-old face brightened with possibility. "Are you writing about me?"

"Yes, as a matter of fact I am!" Dan smirked as he set his brother up for embarrassment.

David's face beamed, and he jumped up and down. "Cool!"

Dan seized the moment. "My English teacher, Mrs. Thomas, instructed us to write a paper about our biggest pet peeve, and I chose you."

David's eager smile faded. His shoulders slumped, his face crumpled, and he fled to his room. Dan sighed heavily and returned to his paper.

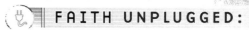 **FAITH UNPLUGGED:**

You are probably influencing someone whether you think you are or not. Someone who is looking for a role model is watching you.

"My biggest pet peeve," he wrote, "is my little brother, David Isaiah Morris. Despite being only eight years old, he is annoying beyond his years. For eight years, he has refined his craft through inexhaustible creativity and endless repetition. David has become a master of irritation. He is a sculptor of frustration, an artist of nuisance, and a poet of exasperation."

Dan's fingers soared across the keyboard. If only he could have typed this fast in computer class. Dan didn't consider himself a talented writer. But as he typed, he knew tonight was different. He was creating his masterpiece, for he had found his motivation.

"Like every creative genius, David's art flows from his inspiration. I'm David's stimulus, his subject, and his canvas. Through me, to me, and on me, he has produced acts of annoyance beyond compare. His works include 'Follow My Brother Everywhere,' 'When a Girl Calls,' 'The Most Painful Sound,' and the ever popular 'Can I Come Too?' I'll attempt to examine and explain each of these pieces."

Dan paused and reviewed his work with pride. As he smiled, he heard a gentle knock on his door. *Now what does he want?* he thought to himself. He heard another knock. "Come in already!" he snapped and glanced toward the door, only to see his mother enter. "Sorry, Mom. I thought you were my little monster. I think you call him David."

"Daniel James Morris." Three names always preceded a lecture.

"Oh, Mom, not now. I'm in the middle of writing a paper."

"That's what I came to talk to you about," she said calmly. "I heard your little brother crying in his room just a few minutes ago. He told me about your paper."

"Well, it's true! He is my biggest pet peeve. Do you want me to lie?" Dan stopped just short of smiling at his best argument to date.

"No, I don't want you to lie. I want you to think about something while you're writing." She ignored Dan's lame attempts to communicate that he didn't want to hear it. "Will you do that for me?"

Taking advantage of the opportunity to end the discussion quickly and return to his art, he nodded.

"In your paper, I want you to try to answer the question why. Why does your brother do all the things that he does? Why does he follow you, mimic you, and interrupt you?"

"Mom, that's easy," he replied without hesitation, "it's 'cause he's a criminal mastermind sent to torture me."

"Dan!" his mother responded sharply.

"I'm serious. He derives pleasure from my suffering."

"You and I both know that isn't the answer. You know why he does it. You just don't want to accept it because of what that means for you."

Touché! Her well-directed arrow hit its target. She allowed the truth to seep in before finishing. "He looks up to you. Honestly, sometimes I don't even know why. I love you to death, Dan, but nevertheless, when it comes to your brother, your attitude shocks me. I'm going to go now. Good luck on your paper." The door closed softly behind her. She left Dan with his thoughts and the words on the screen in front of him.

 ## FAITH LINK:

Jesus, help me set an example for others as you have set an example for me. Help me to be a role model who points others to you.

 ## POWER UP:

Have you ever thought about the influence you have on others? Consider people in your family, as well as your friends, teachers, coaches, classmates, teammates, neighbors, church members, and coworkers. God has given you an amazing opportunity to be an example for each of them, whether younger or older. In the same way others have modeled God's ways to you, you can model them for those who look up to you. Take responsibility for the influence that God has given you. Set an example for others to follow toward Jesus.

LIFE'S TOO BEAUTIFUL

Dreams

DOWNLOAD:

Delight yourself in the LORD and he will give you the desires of your heart. Psalm 37:4 NIV

Peter Brown walked into his first meeting of the year with Mr. O'Connor right after lunch on Friday, two weeks into the school year. Peter was the third Brown to pass through Mr. O's office. The guidance counselor, whose Irish heritage occasionally slipped into in his speech, had really helped his older siblings navigate through their decision-making processes. Both of them had ended up at Ivy League schools. His brother attended Dartmouth; his sister graced Columbia. Peter was proud of them both, but he didn't want to follow their path, and that was about all he knew. He was excited to talk to Mr. O, but apprehensive, because he simply had no clue about his future.

"Mr. Brown!" Mr. O'Connor exclaimed from behind his messy desk. "Good to see you! Come on in and have a seat. How is that family of yours?"

"They're doing well, Mr. O'Connor. Parker finished his undergrad degree at Dartmouth in May. Now he's enrolled at Boston University for a masters in counseling. I think he might be eyeing your job."

Mr. O chuckled loudly.

"And Natasha is still at Columbia. She loves it!"

"Excellent. I'm glad to hear that. More important, I'm glad you're here. I've been looking forward to talking to you about your plans. How's everything coming along?"

"Great," Peter lied. His eyes scanned the floor, as if looking for an escape hatch.

Mr. O'Connor played along. "I see, Peter. It sounds like you have it all figured out then, eh?" He crossed his arms and waited.

"Pretty much, I guess."

"'Pretty much, I guess,'" Mr. O'Connor repeated in mock gruffness. "Oh, that sounds very reassuring, Peter. Since we have at least an hour together, indulge me for a little while. Tell me about those plans of yours." A wily smile developed at the corners of his mouth, peeking out from under his bushy beard.

FAITH UNPLUGGED:

Whatever your dream, consider that God might have given it to you.

"Well, they're kind of complicated. I don't want to waste your time with a long explanation."

"Waste my time? Nonsense, lad. I get paid to listen to complicated explanations." Mr. O chuckled and paused. "Let me guess." He placed a finger on his temple. "You've got no plans yet because you have no idea what you'd like to do. Or maybe you do know, but you don't know how your family might respond. Am I right?"

Peter's mouth fell open. Mr. O had read him like a book. He wanted to speak but waited, trying to choose his words.

Mr. O's face burst forth in a smile. "Peter, it's OK. You're hardly alone. The majority of students who sit in that chair are as confused as you. And just like them, you're not as lost as you might think," he said with a wink.

"What do you mean?"

"Have you given any thoughts to your schooling and career?"

"Of course I have," Peter replied.

"I thought as much. And what are you thinking?"

"Well, my mom wants me to go to an Ivy League school and study premed. She always wanted to have a doctor in the family. Not that she wants me to be a doctor for the money, though; I think she wants free advice. She's kind of paranoid about diseases."

Mr. O chuckled again.

"My dad, on the other hand, would love for one of us to take over the family business. So he's pushing me to get an MBA. And obviously, my siblings are like recruiters for Dartmouth and Columbia. They don't care what I study; they just want me to attend their school. A couple of my friends want me to go with them to UMass. Mr. Wilson suggested I pursue engineering because I'm good at calculus and physics."

"Stop there," Mr. O'Connor interrupted, holding up his hand. "As well intentioned as all of those people might be, I'm not interested in what they fancy you should do. I want to know what you dream about."

"Honestly, Mr. O, I really *am* unsure what to do."

"Unsure or unwilling?"

"What do you mean?" Peter asked.

"Sometimes we are unsure about what we want to do. Other times, we're unwilling to follow our dreams because we're afraid— afraid of either failing or disappointing a loved one by listening to our hearts rather than theirs. What you need to understand, Peter, is that deep inside, every one of those people wants you to be happy and do something you enjoy. Life is too beautiful to spend the majority of our time hating it. So are you unsure or unwilling?"

Peter sat, uncomfortable in the silence following Mr. O's question. "Unwilling, I guess. I mean, I'm not scared of failing or even of disappointing people. I think I'm more afraid of people's comments, their ridicule, actually. I'm worried that people will think I'm being foolish and irresponsible. Does that make sense?"

"Of course it makes sense. Your family values being sensible, and you believe your dream is a little imprudent. It's the nature of a dream to be a little reckless and irresponsible. But notice I didn't say foolish. We must employ wisdom in following our dreams. When we ignore our dreams, I think something in us dies along with them. Peter, let me ask you this: What makes you feel alive?

Peter paused, unsure if he should share his heart. He took a breath. "Mr. O, ever since I was, like, five years old, I've wanted to train dolphins."

As soon as the words escaped his lips, Peter wished he could pull them back. He cringed, half expecting a burst of laughter from his guidance counselor.

Mr. O did laugh, but Peter could tell it was with delight and not from disbelief. "I have always wanted to swim with a dolphin. When you're a dolphin trainer, will you arrange that for me?"

"Definitely," he responded. "But first, where do I go to study dolphins?"

"I'm not sure, but I think you'll need to look into studying marine biology. I would start by looking in Southern California. San Diego, maybe. It's a long way from here, but the beaches are amazing." Mr. O's smile widened as he moved toward his computer. "Let's see here. Marine biology," he murmured as he typed the words into a search engine. Peter jumped out of his chair to see the screen.

 ## FAITH LINK:

Jesus, help me distinguish between my dreams for my life and your dreams for me. If they are the same, give me the courage to follow them.

 ## POWER UP:

What is your dream? Have you ever considered that God might have given you that dream? If he did, will you have the courage to follow through? Often, people abandon their dreams for a life that makes sense. They trade the ideal for the practical. They swap passion for security. They listen to the voices of reason and other people instead of the voice of God. Life is too beautiful and precious to end up hating it or regretting it. Get to know God. Seek God with

all your heart and pursue the dream he placed inside of you.
Following his dream for your life will be your greatest adventure.

WINNING ISN'T EVERYTHING

Competition

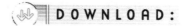 **DOWNLOAD:**

It is obvious what kind of life develops out of trying to get your own way all the time: ... cutthroat competition ... divided homes and divided lives ... the vicious habit of depersonalizing everyone into a rival. Galatians 5:19–21

When Jack Randal and Charlie Swanson met on the first day of middle school, they became instant friends. Jack wore a Seattle Mariners hat. Charlie sported a Chicago Cubs jersey, courtesy of his grandfather, a die-hard fan. Before the first day ended, they made plans to get together once they could secure their parents' permission. The boys simply clicked. For the first time, Charlie found a true friend, and his family found a solution to his relentless requests for someone to play catch with. "Why don't you call Jack?" they'd say.

Their love of the game made their friendship natural, but high school complicated things. During the winter of their sophomore year, the varsity team's starting shortstop, A. J. Gonzales, tore his ACL playing basketball. The coach informed Jack and Charlie that one of them would take his spot in the starting lineup that spring. Initially, they were excited about the possibility of one them playing varsity. It didn't take long to realize that, deep inside, each one wanted to be that player. Both guys created a mental list of reasons why they deserved the starting nod.

Coach Nelson notified Jack and Charlie before practice started that as of this moment they were equals on the depth chart. Jack and Charlie truly were equal. Charlie played a smarter game than Jack and everyone else. He swung an overall better bat and threw with pinpoint accuracy. Jack, on the other hand, brought unmatched speed to the team. He was a contact hitter, so he would make a great leadoff man. His quick glove made him a better defender than Charlie, and he had a stronger but more erratic arm.

By the first ground ball, Jack and Charlie's internal evaluation game became a full-scale, show-no-mercy competition. The two close friends rarely spoke during practice even though they remained warm-up partners. They jockeyed for position in batting practice and field drills to get more repetitions. To make things worse, they took a mental note of every mistake and ignored any success.

Amazingly enough, their on-the-field rivalry stayed on the field. Their close friendship continued, but they talked less about their game and more about the rest of the team. It was similar to freshmen year when Andrea Wilson, a beautiful blonde from Alabama, transferred to the their school. Within two weeks, her accent had them smitten. Most of their interactions with her occurred at school, which meant they were together. At night, they secretly competed for her attention on the phone. Jack and Charlie took the same approach in their pursuit of the southern belle by trying to build a friendship first. It was a short-lived competition. Paul Jacobs skipped building a friendship and went straight to asking her out. She said yes, and the boys had something else in common—a bitter distaste for Paul Jacobs.

Everything went well until after sixth hour, four days before the first game of the season. Jack and Charlie shared a locker. Charlie's fifth-hour class was nearby. Jack had phys ed with Coach Nelson. Coach pulled Jack aside after class and told him his decision. Jack had a long walk to think about what to say to Charlie, who was waiting at the locker for him.

"So what's up, man? How was class?" Charlie asked casually.

Jack stared at his friend. *How did Charlie already know Coach's decision? Maybe he was trying to rub it in by acting cool.* "Don't talk to me!" Jack bellowed, lowering his shoulder to push past his friend.

"Dude?"

"Don't give me that, Charlie," Jack snapped, throwing his books into his bag. "The only reason you got the spot was because you grew up here and everyone else still sees me as an outsider. You didn't beat me out. There was no contest. If there was, I would be starting and not you." He finished his final sentence while slamming the locker shut and shoving his finger in Charlie's chest before stomping down the hallway.

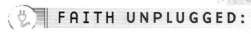

FAITH UNPLUGGED:

When all you care about is winning, you lose.

Andrea Wilson, who remained the object of Jack and Charlie's affection despite her continuing relationship with Paul, witnessed the clash. Approaching a dazed Charlie, she asked, "What was that all about?"

"Baseball," he muttered. "Baseball."

"I should have known," she said, rolling her eyes and walking away.

Though Jack and Charlie remained friends, their relationship never fully recovered. Instead, their friendship ebbed and flowed with their rivalry. Off-season was great. In-season, after Charlie won the starting spot each year, they rarely talked. After Andrea broke up with Paul, they ignored each other. But when Jack and Andrea started dating, Jack and Charlie started hating each other. Charlie hated Jack for winning Andrea. Jack hated Charlie for remaining her friend.

Junior year, Andrea moved back to Alabama. Senior year, their team lost in the state play-offs. Their baseball careers were finished. They walked off the field together. Later that year, the two friends traveled to Chicago for game one of the World Series.

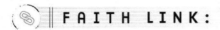

Jack's Seattle Mariners were playing Charlie's Chicago Cubs. The Cubs lost, but, ultimately, friendship won out.

FAITH LINK:

Jesus, I often compete simply to get my own way. I selfishly turn things that you created for me to enjoy with others into a means for selfish gain. In doing so, I realize how much I have lost. Teach me to be more concerned about others than myself.

POWER UP:

Have you ever heard anyone say things like "It's every man for himself" or "Winning is everything" or "You've got to look out for number one"? American life is so competitive. Businesses compete for the market. Individuals and teams compete for championships. Family members compete for each other's time and attention. Students compete for the highest GPA. You compete every day. Competition can be a great motivator for change. However, too often people compete not to improve, but to win. This kind of selfish competition divides friendships, families, communities, teams, churches, and businesses. Have you seen this happen in your life or in the lives of others? Don't get sucked in to this way of living. Instead, put others before yourself and your life will be full.

SIX-PACK OBSESSION

Self-Image

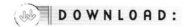

Obsession with self in these matters is a dead end; attention to God leads us out into the open, into a spacious, free life.

Romans 8:6

Church lock-ins lead inevitably to discovery. Staying up all night, eating, running, watching movies. Eventually someone always suggests an innocent game of Truth or Dare.

Girls always choose truth. Guys take the dare. Girls like to talk; guys like to act. Truths scare guys more than dares ever will, even with their potential for causing embarrassment. Guys all hope to hear, "I dare you to kiss ..." And besides, it's easier to back out of a dare than a truth.

"Truth or dare?"

"Truth," Melanie answered.

"All right, Melanie. What part of a guy's body do you find most attractive?"

"That is so easy. Every girl wants a guy with a six-pack. They're so hot."

It's funny how words stick. They resounded in Scott's head every morning when he looked in the mirror. Judging by the talk in the bathroom, he wasn't the only one who remembered. Melanie, after all, was the most popular girl in school. If she said every girl wants a guy with fully defined abs, it must be true.

As far as Scott could tell, chiseled stomachs were all the rage. In the supermarket, shirtless men graced magazine covers. The desktops at the computer lab frequently displayed a shirtless Brad Pitt. Scott's older sister covered her walls with Abercrombie and Fitch advertisements. Even his mom made comments to his dad about his growing gut as opposed to the men on her soap. About the only female in his life who never casually mentioned men's stomachs was his grandmother, and she had lost her sight five years ago.

Puberty was an awkward time for Scott. He was a late bloomer. Most of his friends began their rage into manhood at the beginning of middle school. Scott, on the other hand, spent most of his seventh- and eighth-grade years growing—not hair, not taller, but pudgy. "Why do we gain weight and then get taller?" he often pondered in frustration as he jiggled his small belly in the mirror.

Scott eventually grew, but it happened later than he anticipated, and he didn't achieve the height he'd hoped for. Sure, adding six inches his freshmen year was nice, but he thought every ounce of body fat would disappear too. It went down that way for his friends. Joel had a six-pack. Steve was like a chiseled statue. JT, Chris, and Austin all sported a washboard as well. Scott felt self-conscious around them and their girlfriends. He figured that a six-pack was more of a prerequisite to having a girlfriend than actually asking a girl on a date.

As Christmas vacation ended and summer began its approach, Scott's thoughts strayed further. He continually imagined feeling embarrassed walking behind his friends at the water park where they all bought season passes. Scott pictured a bikini-clad Melanie smiling at the sight of the guys' stomachs, and the smile turning from one of pleasure to courtesy as he passed by. He wondered if his little belly embarrassed his sister, or worse, his mom. She obviously didn't approve of his father's much larger and softer midsection. Ironically, his dad seemed unembarrassed, and maybe even a little proud of his hard-earned spare tire.

Scott decided to start working out and running. He lived about two miles from school, so he decided to run there every morning at six. The head football coach opened the weight room every morning around that time, so he could lift there for free. Showering in the locker rooms was no problem either. All he needed was a ride home after school, which he could get from his sister.

It took a few weeks before Scott could run the entire distance to school without walking, but it was only the end of January, so he had plenty of time. He talked to Coach Duke, who designed a work-out plan for him. On Mondays, Wednesdays, and Fridays he focused on his upper body. On Tuesdays and Thursdays, he worked his legs. He hated Tuesdays and Thursdays, but he eagerly anticipated the daily abdominal exercises Coach had prescribed.

FAITH UNPLUGGED:

Many guys struggle with their body image. And more and more have developed eating disorders. Don't be ashamed to get help just because you think you're the only guy to face this struggle.

By March, people began noticing his changing physique. The guys encouraged him to keep it up. His discipline wowed his family. Occasionally, a pretty girl or two flashed him a smile that was just a little bit bigger. Melanie even grabbed his bicep one day.

"Have you been working out, Scott?"

He could only manage a grin and a shrug of his shoulders as he tried to play cool.

"Keep it up, stud!"

Scott found additional inspiration. He asked Coach to design a more intense workout for him. He decided to start running to *and* from school. Every morning and every night, he would do an excessive number of sit-ups, often pausing to check for any signs of improvement. During the day, he constantly stopped by the restroom to look at himself in the mirror. Working out became the only thing he thought about or talked about. He continued to improve rapidly. His strength increased exponentially, and he breathed easily through his two-mile runs.

When school ended, Scott was in amazing shape. However, like the onset of puberty, it wasn't all he had hoped for. For some reason his stomach didn't look like the rest of his friends' abdomens. He dropped four inches off his waistline and his stomach was super firm and flat. Yet a thin layer still hid the muscles underneath. He could not understand it or accept it.

"I can't go to the water park looking like this," he said to himself, standing shirtless in front of a full-length mirror scrutinizing his body from every angle. Scott could not see his well-developed chest and arms. His V-shaped torso, defined calves, and chiseled face made no difference. From his perspective nothing had changed in five months of hard work. When he looked in the mirror, he saw the chubby junior-high kid sitting in a Truth or Dare circle, listening to Melanie say ...

"Every girl wants a guy with a six-pack. They're so hot."

 ## FAITH LINK:

Jesus, I need your help to see myself the way you see me. Show me if I have problems with my body image, and give me the strength to seek help if I do.

 ## POWER UP:

A lot of people assume that only girls deal with negative self-image issues, but that's not true. Guys are frequently assaulted with images and messages describing how they should look as well. This very well could be the reason that eating disorders are becoming more common in men, why so many amateur and professional athletes give in to using steroids and other performance-enhancing drugs, and why so many young men are increasingly unhappy with their perfectly healthy, normal bodies.

Frequent dieting, excessive exercising, and dissatisfaction with your body might seem normal and harmless, but they can quickly compromise your long-term health. Under extreme circumstances, they can lead to an uncontrollable, life-threatening eating disorder. Common eating disorders include anorexia (self-starvation) and bulimia (self-induced vomiting). If you or anyone you know is struggling with an eating disorder or other body-image issues, take action now. Seek God and professional help. If you think you are in control but others who care about you question that, you are probably not. Don't take any chances. Your health and life are far too valuable.

IN THE WOODS

Pornography

DOWNLOAD:

Don't think you've preserved your virtue simply by staying out of bed. Your heart can be corrupted by lust even quicker than your body. Those leering looks you think nobody notices—they also corrupt. Matthew 5:28

PJ's ten-page English research paper was due in two weeks. He had finally picked a topic yesterday. Sitting at his computer in his room, he researched the history and development of political parties in the United States. His parents' involvement with the Republican Party over the years greatly influenced his decision. He was tired of not being able to contribute to their discussions, and, because of the war, he began questioning his own political beliefs.

PJ visited Google to begin collecting resources. He visited democrats.org and gop.com to read their histories along with a multitude of other sites the search browser provided. A couple of hours into his research, he stood to stretch. He walked around his room a few times and began to remember the first time.

He was ten years old. His friend Rusty invited him over to his house to play. PJ loved Rusty's house because it backed up to a forest. Most of their childhood adventures took place in the trees. They played countless games of hide-and-seek with the rest of the neighborhood kids. The forest was the ideal location for staging battles between good and evil. They fantasized about being Jedi Knights. When they were eight, Rusty's dad built them the most amazing fort they had ever seen. At ten, they began spending the night out there, exploring the grounds by flashlight.

Rusty found the box and called PJ to come and look. Apparently, they were not the only ones hiding in the woods. Before their innocent and curious eyes lay a cardboard box filled with *Playboy* magazines. They stood there, shining their lights on the discovery for an eternity. A wave of arousal and fear shot through them as they silently debated what to do. The boys made their decision, picking up the box and carrying it back to the fort.

They looked at one magazine at a time, slowly flipping through the pictures in complete awe. The rest of the magazines they hid outside the fort in case one of Rusty's parents came to check on them. It would be easy to hide a single magazine in their sleeping bags, not an entire box. Neither PJ nor Rusty could describe the rush of emotions that first time. They had never felt anything like it before.

 FAITH UNPLUGGED:

Pornography makes objects out of people. It robs them of their humanity and takes yours in the process.

PJ and Rusty vowed never to tell anyone about their newfound treasure. They didn't want to get in trouble, which they guessed would happen. Neither of their parents had ever told them it was wrong; they innately knew. Moreover, the boys didn't want the magazines taken away; their exploration had only begun. There were more pictures to see and others to revisit. That night in the woods, the boys entered a new world of fantasy and adventure.

As they grew up, they returned to the forest frequently. Eventually, they invited other friends to join them. The best nights were the nights when one of their friends saw the magazines for the first time. It was as close as they came to that initial experience. Even though the magazines never delivered what they promised, the hope that they might never faded. PJ and Rusty thought about the pictures constantly, idealizing each experience beyond reality and plotting their next viewing.

They never imagined the life that began that night. At thirteen, the girls in their school became a new realm of fantasy and discussion. A few years later, their parents bought them computers for school, providing them with unlimited, unfiltered, unsupervised Internet access. PJ and Rusty no longer had to visit the woods. Before long, the magazines that captured their attention and the fort that concealed them withered away for lack of attention.

Rusty and PJ's friendship changed as well. They remained close, but spent less time together. The encounters that connected them so deeply to each other became much more private. When they did hang out, they spent most of their time exchanging Web addresses or comparing notes about their physical experiences with their girlfriends. Other than the few friends they allowed into the fort, they kept their vow to one another. Their pornographic adventures, though no longer hidden in the forest, remained very much in the dark.

Recently, PJ had waved good-bye to the pictures. They simply no longer satisfied his cravings. He really liked his girlfriend and found her attractive, but she could not quench his thirst either. PJ felt constantly frustrated. He had become a powder keg, blowing up at the smallest irritations. A few times, his anger turned to violence. PJ smashed a hole in his wall when his computer crashed. Another time during a pickup game at the park, another teenager hacked him as he went for layup. PJ lost control, landing three or four punches before his friends restrained him. He didn't have to search long before finding temporary gratification for his dissatisfaction in downloadable films.

As he paced around his room remembering the first time, his computer called him back. He tried to fight the urge. He needed to work on his paper. His last English paper earned him a D because he could not stay away. Every time he told himself "I'll just go to one site" or "I'll only look for a minute two," the black hole sucked him in for hours. PJ used to be an above-average student; now he could barely pass his classes.

"What's the point?" he said with a sigh, surrendering to the temptation. "I might as well just get it over with." PJ closed his door and sat down in front of his computer. But he paused for a moment. "God," he prayed, "please help me with this problem. It's got hold of me and I can't seem to fight it anymore. Please help me figure out what I should do."

PJ felt a weight drop from his shoulders as an idea entered his mind. He got up from the computer, left his room, and found his parents in the living room. "Mom? Dad? I need to talk to you about something."

FAITH LINK:

Jesus, help me to understand how big of a deal pornography really is. Forgive me and cleanse my mind of the images I have seen. I commit to lead a pure life, but I can't do it alone. Give me the power to resist temptation. Bring people into my life who can keep me accountable.

POWER UP:

Pornography separates sex and marriage. It promotes the using of people's sexuality for your own pleasure without any sense of love or commitment to them. Pornography turns people who Jesus says are worth dying for into objects of obsession and self-gratification. Objectifying people is evil and destructive to everyone involved. Avoid looking at pornography at all costs. If you already have, do whatever it takes to stop. Throw away your magazines and videos. Move your computer out of your room to a public place and install the best filter you can find. Ask your father, pastor, or friend to pray with you and hold you accountable. Most importantly, turn to Jesus.

OLD FRIENDS

Witnessing

DOWNLOAD:

We're Christ's representatives. God uses us to persuade men and women to drop their differences and enter into God's work of making things right between them. We're speaking for Christ himself now: Become friends with God; he's already a friend with you. 2 Corinthians 5:20

Everything changed when Patrick Halloway found God.

Word spread quickly around the school about his decision: "Did you hear about Patrick?"

"I heard he's become, like, totally religious or something. Is that true?"

"Yep."

"I was wondering why I never saw him on the weekends anymore."

"Never thought Patrick Halloway would find God."

"Me neither."

Patrick's heart-change propelled him to disconnect completely from his old way of life. Summer vacation provided the means to do so. Since he was no longer partying, Patrick rarely saw his friends. The youth group at the church he attended became his new social cluster. It was a different culture. His church friends spoke a distinctive language. They listened to their own music and applied a new standard to movies, television, and clothing. They didn't drink. They didn't smoke. They didn't have sex. The world

Patrick had known was dissimilar to this new one in every imaginable way—even the jokes were different. Patrick plunged himself into this new society.

The school year started with greetings and questions. "Patrick, what's up, man? Where you been all summer? We missed you."

How do I respond? he wondered, hesitating. *I missed them, but not the life.* "I've been hanging out at church all summer, but I missed you, too. How was your summer?" became his common answer.

Why did he hesitate? his friends thought, puzzled. The uneasiness of the initial interchanges increased with time. He felt noticeably uncomfortable when his old friends talked about last weekend's party. They were

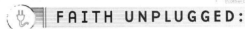 **FAITH UNPLUGGED:**

Jesus has placed his reputation on you. How you live gives people a picture of what they think God is like. Therefore, live a life of love.

equally unnerved when he mentioned anything about God or church. Eventually, Patrick sat closer to the front on bus trips to avoid hearing the weekend stories. He ate lunch either alone or with his church friends. Instead of using the locker room, he often went home to shower after practice. He still smiled, said hello, and asked about the day. His participation in school events, groups, and teams stayed the same. Nevertheless, his disconnection from his old lifestyle became publicly clear.

Occasionally, his attempts to elude his past and everything associated with it failed. It was impossible to escape completely. He overheard conversations and accidentally found himself in others. Patrick still didn't know how to react. The last thing he wanted to do was join in and unintentionally communicate that he approved of their behavior. Normally, he froze. His body language created a tension that everyone could feel. He unsuccessfully tried to bring God into the discussion quite a few times. In the end, he opted to walk away.

Oddly, it was Toby, who always came across as a slacker, who seemed to understand best. And Will, one of Patrick's best friends, had the hardest time with Patrick's attempts at witnessing.

"I'm tired of feeling like I have to watch my words around him," Will vented to a group of friends one Saturday night. "It's ridiculous. Last year, he was right here drinking with us. Now all he does is make me feel guilty about it. He had the nerve to try to talk to me about God last Thursday. He knows how I feel about that stuff, and he did it anyway. I'm sick of it."

"I'm with you," joined Marcus. "The other day a group of us were planning for tonight. He walked up, said hi, and asked us what we were doing. So, I told him. He just stood there looking down at his feet. What does he want me to do—lie? Wait! I'm not supposed to do that, either." Everyone laughed.

"I just stopped caring," added Gail. "Seriously, let him walk away. I don't care anymore. I'm not going to change who I am just because he found Jesus. If he walks up to my table when I'm talking about partying with Heath, or whatever, I'll keep right on talking."

The group looked at Toby, as if expecting him to join in on the complaints about Patrick. But he said nothing, and the others kept on.

The group's discussion carried on for over an hour as others joined in sharing stories about their contacts with Patrick and his church friends. Everyone was boiling by the end of the night— Will's anger being the most apparent.

The next week at school, Will talked to Patrick. Patrick sat down next to Will's table at lunch. Sensing a chance to make a point, Will loudly began talking about last weekend's party. He continued for a while, periodically glancing toward Patrick, monitoring his reactions. The longer he talked, the louder and dirtier he talked. Will's intentions were obvious to everyone, including Patrick. When Patrick stood to leave, Will went off.

"Hey, Halloway! Where are you going? What's the matter? Did I say something that bothered you?"

Patrick stopped. "Come on, Will," he said, hoping to defuse the situation.

"No, you come on!" Will yelled, rising to his feet. "I'm tired of you walking away like you're too good for us and the rest of us feeling guilty about it. A year ago, you were my friend, and we were doing all of this stuff together. You went off, found God, and now you think you're better than the rest of us. You're nothing but an arrogant, judgmental hypocrite. I'm sick of all your religious crap."

Will stomped away, and Patrick just stood there, speechless. He never imagined such a scenario or intended for this to happen. He wasn't trying to judge anyone; he was just trying to live the way God wanted him to. He had been afraid his old friends would drag him into his old ways.

Toby rose from the table and walked toward Patrick. "Dude, don't worry too much about Will. He'll get over it."

"Well, do I come across like I think I'm too good for my old friends?"

"Maybe a little, dude," Toby said. "Look, I can tell you've changed, but maybe you need to chill out a little and just let people be who they are instead of getting all weird when they talk about their lives." Toby punched Patrick lightly on the arm. "After all, even Jesus hung out with the sinners."

Patrick laughed in amazement at what he was hearing from Toby. "Yeah, maybe you're right."

Toby laughed too. "See? You'll be all right."

 **FAITH LINK:**

Jesus, thank you for setting things right between you and me. Thank you for entrusting me with your message of reconciliation. Show me how to live to best represent you to the world, and forgive me for the times I have not done so. Please send your Spirit to empower me.

POWER UP:

In a radical move, when Jesus ascended into heaven, he entrusted his message to his followers. If you are one of his followers, he has given you the power to live as his representative on the earth. If you claim affiliation with him, others are watching your life and making decisions about God based on what they see. Thankfully, Jesus didn't leave us alone. He sent his Spirit to empower us to represent him well. Jesus makes it clear in his teachings that the best way to carry his reputation is in a life of love. He lived among the regular people of his day and let his light shine on all of them. Too often people feel that Jesus is against them because of the actions of Christians. If this has happened to you, know that Jesus loves you and desperately wants a relationship with you. Please don't let the actions of others prevent you from experiencing his love for you. If you have represented Jesus in an unloving way, whether intentionally or not, humble yourself and ask those people for their forgiveness.

YOU AND I
ARE PEOPLE

C h u r c h

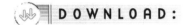

DOWNLOAD:

The way God designed our bodies is a model for understanding our lives together as a church: every part dependent on every other part, the parts we mention and the parts we don't, the parts we see and the parts we don't. If one part hurts, every other part is involved in the hurt, and in the healing. If one part flourishes, every other part enters into the exuberance. You are Christ's body—that's who you are! You must never forget this. Only as you accept your part of that body does your "part" mean anything.   1 Corinthians 12:25–27

On Saturday nights Paul often met a bunch of his friends from church at the movies. This Saturday he arrived early; it was his turn to buy the tickets in case of a sellout. Everyone had given him their money on Wednesday night after the youth meeting. While he waited for the others, he saw Abe with his friend Bruce. Paul had met Bruce only once. It was three months ago when Abe brought him to church. He hadn't seen Abe since then.

"Hey, guys," Paul said, grabbing their attention. "What's going on?"

"Hey, Paul, how are you?" Abe responded, veering his path toward Paul. The two exchanged their usual man hug and shake. "You remember Bruce, right?"

"Of course, how you doin'?" Paul said, stretching out his hand. The two shook, but didn't man-hug. After all, they had met only once before.

"Great," Bruce said. Recognizing that Paul wanted to talk to Abe, he said, "Abe, why don't you stay here. I'll go get in line for tickets." By this time, the line had grown considerably.

"Are you sure?" Abe asked. Bruce nodded and walked toward the box office.

"How've you been? I haven't seen you in forever," Paul began.

"I'm good. Things have been busy at school and at work. You know how that goes."

"I figured something like that when I didn't see you at church or youth group."

"Yeah," Abe said, his eyes looking away from Paul toward the ticket window then down at his feet before reengaging eye contact.

Paul guessed there was more to Abe's absence than busyness. Since he was unsure when he might have another chance, he decided to delve deeper. "Abe, what's going on—for real?"

Abe smiled as people do when they're uncertain how to respond and want to lighten the mood while they think. Finally, he said, "For real?"

"Definitely, I want you to shoot straight with me."

"Honestly, I've stopped going to church completely and I'm not planning on coming back."

"Really?" Paul responded. "Why?"

"Well, you remember a few months ago when I brought Bruce with me to church. Afterwards, I asked him what he thought and we talked about it for quite a while. The conversation really changed my opinion when I looked at the church from an outside perspective."

"What did he say?" Paul inquired.

"It wasn't as much about what he said as how he felt. For starters, Bruce goes to school at Eisenhower with a bunch of other people from the youth group. Bruce has a bad reputation. He's made a lot of mistakes. We became friends through work.

But anyway, I asked him if he wanted to come to church and he said sure. The moment we walked in, the other Eisenhower students stared at him and started whispering. Not one of them said hi to him the whole night. In fact, I think you were the only person who actually introduced yourself."

"No way," Paul said, wanting it not to be true.

"It gets worse. By the end of the night, everyone else was being all standoffish and unfriendly too. You could tell they were talking about him. At first I didn't think that much about it, but when he mentioned it later, I knew he was telling the truth. I didn't know what to say."

Abe shrugged. "I think he was starting to open up to God, and then he came to church. It crushed what little

FAITH UNPLUGGED:

Be who you want the church to be.

hope I saw. I decided that night I wanted nothing to do with church, at least that church. Everyone—except maybe you—is so judgmental, hypocritical, and cliquey. I hate it. It's so frustrating."

"I'm so sorry that happened," Paul said. "I understand how you feel."

"You do?" Abe wondered.

"Yep. Unfortunately. Been there and done that myself," Paul answered. Only a year or so ago, he'd quit coming to church for a similar reason. What ultimately made the difference was that a group of kids from the church took the time and effort to reach out to him, and Paul had been a fixture at church ever since then.

Paul paused for a moment, unsure if Abe might be open to his idea. "Why don't you and Bruce come to the movie with us? These guys are all cool, and maybe we could sort of make it up to Bruce for ... what happened, you know?"

"I'm not sure ..." Abe started. "Let me ask Bruce."

To Abe's surprise, Bruce agreed.

The next Sunday, Abe decided to give church another chance. *And maybe,* he thought, *Bruce will try it again sometime too.*

FAITH LINK:

Jesus, thank you for bringing me into your family. Thank you for connecting me to a community of fellow believers and allowing me to express your love for others. Help me to be an active participant rather than a passive complainer. Help me to become a reflection of you in my church family.

POWER UP:

People often think of the church as a mere building. But people are the church. You are the church. The church is simply the collection of God's people—his family. One writer compared the church to a human body. Everything is interconnected and interdependent. Every person plays a role, and every role is important. What part can you play? Are you filling your role? Are you actively serving in your local faith community, or are you only there to be entertained?

Every local faith community has things they do well and things they are trying to improve. The question is, how are you spending your time? Are you talking about the problems or are you becoming a part of the solution?

If you are not involved in a local community of believers, take the first steps to become involved. Faith was never meant to be done alone; it was designed to be lived out in community with other followers. You need them and they need you.

CULTURE CLASS

Media

DOWNLOAD:

Watch your step. Use your head. Make the most of every chance you get. These are desperate times! Don't live carelessly, unthinkingly. Make sure you understand what the Master wants.
Ephesians 5:15-17

Students were buzzing with excitement Monday as they filed into Mr. Foster's American History class to find "Pop Culture" scrawled across the chalkboard. Thus began five exhilarating days of talking about movies, music, television, sports, advertising, and even comic books in class. The educational adventure began with the students sharing their favorite films, bands, and ads. "Why is that your favorite?" and "What is the core message?" became the focal questions.

"Jeff, why do you like *Spider-Man* so much? Please let your answer be something deeper than Kirsten Dunst," Mr. Foster pleaded, looking over to a smiling Kale whose answers were profoundly limited.

"I don't know. I never really thought about it that much."

"Precisely, as Americans we don't think. We don't test. We don't examine. We passively accept anything entertaining without question," Mr. Foster responded overenthusiastically. "We spend millions of dollars and hours watching movies, reading magazines, and listening to music that we don't really understand. Our only justification for the expense is that we liked it or it was funny. If you think about it for just a second, it's actually quite absurd."

The next day in class Mr. Foster, after a brief talk on content analysis, split the class into groups of three. Each group's task was to analyze from memory an assigned piece of pop culture for messages involving race, ethnicity, gender, family, sexuality, and American nationalism.

"For example," he said, "what do the *American Pie* movies communicate about teenage sexuality in America?" Most of the class laughed when they heard the movie mentioned. "It obviously communicates that teenage sexuality is lighthearted and funny. Unfortunately, many teenagers' sexual experiences are painful and confusing." The class stopped laughing.

Twenty minutes later, the groups presented their discoveries. One group noticed an overwhelming number of messages ranging from the dangers of overindulgence to the healing power of forgiveness in the movie *Charlie and the Chocolate Factory.* Jeff's group shared insights into racism they found in the *Harry Potter* movies. A group of three girls realized that the television shows they were watching communicated subtle negative images about parents and adults. Kale and his friends looked at reality television and decided it might not be completely realistic; after all, someone edits what we see. The final two groups looked more closely at the songs stuck in their heads. When they wrote out the lyrics, they hadn't realized how overtly the songs promoted sexual activity among teens.

Wednesday in class, Mr. Foster taught about the history of pop culture. Specifically, he discussed the changing public opinions about race, ethnicity, gender, family, sexuality, and nationalism. He illustrated the transitions masterfully, utilizing a wide range of well-known books, films, shows, songs, and more. It was one of those rare moments when students hang on to their teacher's every word.

"Keeping in mind all that we have learned, does the media lead pop culture or does it follow pop culture? Or in other words, do

movies, music, television shows, and other forms of media influence culture or are they influenced by culture?"

"I think the media follows the culture," Holly answered first.

"Me, too" her friend Kate chimed in.

A momentary silence fell as the rest of the class continued to
think.

"Kale, what do you think?" Mr. Foster asked.

"It definitely follows. No question."

Slowly, almost everyone in the class added their agreement.

"OK. Why do you think that's true?"

"Well, Mr. Foster, take the
gender issue you talked about
yesterday," Holly began. "You
mentioned the changing roles
of men and women in society,
right?" She waited for confir-
mation before continuing.

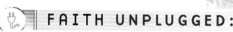 **FAITH UNPLUGGED:**

What you see and hear influences
how you think, which affects who you
are.

"Yes."

"Well, I know a couple of moms who were working outside of
the home even before I remember seeing it on TV, including my
mom. So when I saw it on TV, it wasn't shocking. I had already
experienced it, it was already normal."

"OK. Does anyone else have an explanation?"

"No, we like Holly's," Kale declared.

"You know that you're presenting an argument based solely on
personal experience, right? Have you considered that other forms
of media other than television might have led the charge in the
changing of gender roles? Have you considered what affected your
family and caused your mom to want or need to work outside the
home?"

The class fell silent again. Mr. Foster smiled before asking his
next question.

"For the sake of discussion, let's follow Holly's lead and make
the question more personal. Are you personally leading media or
following media? Or in other words, are you influenced by what

you see and hear, or do the things you see and hear simply put words to your reality?"

"If it's either of the two, it's the second option," Jeff answered. "There are times a song or movie or something like that really connects with what I'm personally experiencing. Most of the time, I would say media neither influences me nor connects to my life."

"Neither? Class, do you agree with Jeff's statement?" Most of the class nodded.

Kale added, "They're just movies and songs, Mr. Foster."

"Thank you, Kale, for the reminder," Mr. Foster replied jokingly. He continued, "I was beginning to think they contained actual ideas about life and the world, but thank you for enlightening me." The class tentatively laughed.

"Let me ask you another question. Do your friends influence you?"

"Yes," the class echoed in universal agreement.

"OK. Let me create a scenario for you, and you tell me if it's true. Let us imagine that you're frustrated with me for some reason. We will say I gave you an undeserved bad grade. In your frustration, you vent to your best friend. Your words about me influence their opinion of me, correct?"

"Correct."

"Now let's imagine that friend already felt frustrated with me. Could your frustration coupled with their frustration lead you both to feeling angry and vengeful toward me?"

"Yeah, it happens all the time," Jeff responded back.

"Good. Now let us imagine you're furious with your parents for some reason, any reason. You storm into your room, slamming the door, and turn on your stereo. You start listening to a heavy, dark, and angry band whose lyrics relate to what you're experiencing with your parents. Does it affect you? Or could that music act in the same way your friends do, pushing you further and deeper than you were before?"

No one answered. Mr. Foster let this question sink in, and then he concluded, "We like to believe that the media doesn't affect us in any way. Mainly, because we don't want to acknowledge that something could influence us without our permission. We live with a false sense of total control, and we like the illusion. When we say something is 'just a movie' or 'just a song' or 'just anything,' we perpetuate that false reality. We downplay things to justify participation and in effect allow those things to have an even greater influence.

"Our lack of humility or our inability to admit that media can sway us leads us to a passive acceptance of everything. We just inhale everything without ever thinking about what it's saying or how it could persuade us. Hopefully, by the end of the week, you'll become much more honest about yourselves and analytical about all forms of media."

 ## FAITH LINK:

Jesus, I have lived carelessly, without thinking about what I watch or how I watch it. I have done the same thing with what I listen to and how I listen. I like the idea of doing whatever I want without consequences, but it's not true. Help me to think critically, and in humility, watch my step.

 ## POWER UP:

How many messages do you hear each day? How many messages do you see? Think about the amount of music you listen to, the number of TV shows you watch, the quantity of advertisements you look at, or the number of movies you see. Thousands of messages and images fill your brain every day. Each communicates something specific. Most of them try to persuade you to believe certain things. All of them hope to influence you in some way or another. And they do. Most people passively receive all of the messages without thinking twice about them. In doing so, they allow things that are not true or good to affect them. Do you do the same? Think about the number of song lyrics, movie quotes, and commercials you can recall. They are imprinted in your mind, affecting how you think and how you live. Commit to live differently. Instead of passively accepting everything you see, think critically about the messages contained in what most people call entertainment. Ask God to help you see the truth.

INTO THE LIGHT

Homosexuality

DOWNLOAD:

I'll take the hand of those who don't know the way, who can't see where they're going. I'll be a personal guide to them, directing them through unknown country. I'll be right there to show them what roads to take, make sure they don't fall into the ditch. These are the things I'll be doing for them—sticking with them, not leaving them for a minute. Isaiah 42:16

The terrifying feeling of having no control drove him to tears. Covered in sweat, lying on the bed in the corner of his darkened room, he cried. Bobby had raced home after school, wanting nothing more than to be alone even though solitude scared him. He managed to hide his emotions through the last hour of the day until he reached his driveway. A cruel joke triggered today's emotional explosion, but the eruptions were common for Bobby. Most of the time they needed no spark.

Bobby's friends had been gathered in the hallway between classes; he joined them as usual. They were plotting to pull another prank on Ronald. Unfortunately for Ronald, he is the school's easiest and most common target. Ronald carries a large portion of his excess weight in his chest, giving him the appearance of a man with breasts. He laughs and speaks at levels usually associated with women. In addition, Ronald loves drama and music. The fact that he is good only makes things worse for him.

Never having been on a date with a girl, though he has asked, sealed his fate. Everyone had decided for him—

"Ronald is gay."

The guys were debating which one of them would "goose" Ronald in the hallway before mockingly asking him about his weekend plans. The moment Bobby walked into the conversation, the guys said, "Bobby will do it!" This was an easy and unanimous decision for the rest of the group since none of them actually had to do anything. They could simply watch and laugh.

"What am I doing this time?" he asked, exchanging a few handshakes and high fives with his friends and teammates.

"Grabbing Ronald's butt and asking him out this weekend!" Ryan informed him.

The comment caught him unprotected. He briefly hesitated before responding, "No way. I'm not doing it." He unsuccessfully tried to laugh in the middle of his sentence to lighten the atmosphere.

"Come on, Bobby. It'll be hilarious," chimed Kenny.

"Don't you think we should lay off of Ronald for a while?" Bobby suggested.

"Why are you always sticking up for that faggot?" Ryan snapped, frustrated by Bobby's resistance. "Are you trying to be the homo's friend or something more?"

Bobby hesitated. He felt attacked. He felt exposed. He needed to respond quickly and effectively. Finally, he found the words to deflect his embarrassment. "I just don't want to grab the guy's butt, but you seem really interested and emotionally connected to the idea."

It was Ryan's turn to freeze. He hesitated only shortly before coming back with a joke. "I just can't help it. I love that big booty." The way he said the words helped draw a laugh from everyone but Bobby. The bell rang and everyone took off. Bobby moved more slowly than the rest. He began to sweat as breathing became more difficult.

Ryan's accusation resounded in his ears as he rested on his bed, staring at his ceiling. Fear took over and the questions drowned out Ryan's voice. *Did he know? How? Was it something I said or something I did? Maybe Ryan could just tell by looking at me? Do I look gay? What if he says something to the other guys? What if he already did? Maybe they all know? Maybe they can all tell.*

Fear gave way to confusion. *But I'm not gay. Am I? I don't think I am. I don't want to be. But how else do you explain my thoughts? Why else would I look at guys sometimes? Why else would I look at magazine covers with guys on the front? But I look at girls and magazines with girls on the cover too. I look at girls and think about girls more often than I do guys. I want to think about girls. I can't control the thoughts about guys. They just happen, even when I don't want them. Maybe that means that deep inside I like guys, but I don't want to like guys so I try to force myself to like girls. But I don't have to force myself to like girls.*

FAITH UNPLUGGED:

There is a way out of everything through Jesus, who loves you, accepts you, frees you, and makes you whole.

Bobby remembered the first time he had begun to have these worries. A sharply dressed and handsome man drew his attention one night at the mall. Bobby stared at him without thinking a thing. Then suddenly he stopped and looked away. Immediately, a question flew into his mind: *Why were you staring at that guy? Are you gay?* The question frightened and confused him.

Over the next two years, the question would torment him and drive him to explore. When he could not shake the thought, he decided to test it. He researched online a few things about the nature of homosexuality; the scientific arguments only confused him more. Bobby looked briefly at a pornographic Web site, which proved to be equally confusing. He experienced an emotional rush from doing something he knew he shouldn't, while feeling ashamed at the same time. Then he found a gay and lesbian chat room. Everyone was nice and helpful as he tried to sort out his thoughts. Eventually, when he knew it was safe, he tried looking at other guys to see if he could feel anything. Most of the time, he felt nothing. A few times he thought a guy was attractive or good looking, but he didn't feel *attracted* to him. He wondered if that was normal or not.

He wondered a lot, usually when he was alone. Bobby desperately fought to keep his thoughts a secret. The only conversations he had were online in the chat room where he could remain anonymous. Their acceptance of him floored him. He doubted he could find the same acceptance anywhere else. His interactions with his friends and others, who continually made fun of homosexuals, confirmed this suspicion. The pranks and jokes fueled his desire for secrecy, preventing him from talking to people who could possibly help.

The longer the question continued and his search for answers remained unfulfilled, the more confusing life became for Bobby. He had difficulty asking girls on dates or to dances because of the internal awkwardness he felt. He avoided showering in the locker room, unsure what might happen there. Bobby withdrew into himself, talking less and thinking more. He experienced a depressing combination of fear, loneliness, exhaustion, and shame.

Fear won today's battle as his tears continued to fall. Bobby wanted to be normal and wondered if he was. He longed for this to end. He wished for someone to talk with, someone he could trust. He yearned for help and for answers, but he knew finding them meant telling. Bobby feared telling as much as he feared what would happen if he never did.

As the tears slowed, Bobby knew he needed to make a decision. His first option was to continue to live with these distressing thoughts until they either disappeared or turned into something more. His second option was to tell someone he could trust. He weighed the options. Bobby decided he had felt out of control long enough; he needed to talk to someone. At least then he would feel like he was doing something instead of simply allowing his fears to control him.

FAITH LINK:

Jesus, I have kept my struggle in the dark for too long. In the dark, it only gains strength, but in your light, I believe I can walk toward freedom. Honestly, I'm scared to tell anyone because I'm not sure about the response I'll get. Please show me the people whom I can trust and who can help. Give me the strength to tell them and continue to pursue you.

POWER UP:

Homosexuality carries so many stigmas and stereotypes that it fills people with fear. If you have ever struggled with thoughts or temptations, you have dealt with the fear of the questions it creates and the fear of wondering how people would treat you if they knew. The fear of homosexuality prevents many people from seeking help. Having thoughts or feeling temptation doesn't make you a homosexual. However, feeding those thoughts and temptations by hiding them and giving into them could easily lead you down a painful and confusing road. Jesus loves you and he wants to help. Let him take you by the hand and lead you into his light, where you will find peace and comfort. Commit to continue to follow him all the way through what could be a long but important process.

DOING TIME

Punishment

DOWNLOAD:

The Lord disciplines those he loves, and he punishes everyone he accepts as a son. Hebrews 12:6 NIV

The best day of Raymond's life was the day he got arrested. Raymond tried shoplifting a CD from Best Buy. His friends had encouraged him to do it. And he almost got away with it but had set off the alarm on his way out of the store. He thought about running. When his friends saw what happened, they took off. But Raymond stayed put. He stood alone as the store manager escorted him inside to wait for the police. Calling his parents to the police station felt worse than the arrest. He could not erase their disappointed and worried looks as they walked through the doors.

Since it was his first offense, the judge went easy on him. He sentenced Raymond to twenty-five hours of community service, which he needed to complete in four weeks.

"That's over six hours a week. How am I going to manage that?" he asked his parents the next morning over breakfast.

"Actually, it's going to be more like twelve and a half hours per week. Your dad and I feel the judge was a little too easy on you, so we signed you up to work fifty hours over the next month. But don't worry, you will have plenty of time since you won't be doing anything else besides school for the next month," his mother said.

Raymond fell silent as he finished his cereal. He thought about all the things he would be missing during that time. It was definitely not worth trying to save twenty bucks by stealing. When he stopped feeling sorry for himself, he asked his parents where he could perform his community service.

"We were hoping the judge would sentence you to community service, so I spent the last week calling different places," his father responded. "I already arranged for you to tutor elementary school kids every day after school. I let the director know how good you are at math."

Just wonderful, he thought. *I get to spend the next month with a bunch of stupid kids who don't know how to do math. This is going to be the worst month of my life.*

That afternoon, his dad picked him up from school. "Where exactly is this place that we're going?" Raymond inquired, a hint of hostility in his voice.

"Over on the west side of town, near Garfield Elementary. There's a day care with an after-school program for older children who have younger siblings that stay there during the day. It's a great program for single parents. I was impressed talking to the director on the phone. His name is Victor. I think you're going to like him."

Raymond was annoyed with his dad's optimism. He decided not to ask him any more questions.

They arrived at the day care around three thirty. "Here we are. Victor is expecting you, so there's no need for me to go inside with you. I'll pick you up at six," his dad said.

"Six?" Raymond groaned.

"That's right, Raymond. Six o'clock is two and a half hours from now. Five days a week at two and a half hours a day times four weeks is fifty hours."

"Dad! I can do the math." He paused and then chuckled. "Otherwise I wouldn't be tutoring these kids!"

His dad smiled. "All right. Six o'clock it is then. Have fun."

Raymond walked in the building where nearly thirty elementary-school-age children were settling into their places. A man came over to meet him. "My name is Victor. I'm the director here. It's a pleasure to meet you," he said, sticking out his hand. Raymond hesitantly shook it. "Let me show you around the place and fill you in on what we need from you."

Raymond was shocked to see so many other high school students and adults. "Are they all doing community-service hours?"

Victor chuckled. "Well, you could say that, I guess."

"What's so funny?"

"Well, they're all doing community-service hours, but none of them are required to do so. Everyone else volunteers their time. This team is here every Tuesday and Thursday. A few of them are here all day."

Raymond's mouth fell open. He could not believe someone would volunteer at a place like this all day. He didn't know whether their service should inspire him or make him pity their lack of a social life.

"Raymond, let me introduce you to Nathan. Nathan is a fifth grader at Garfield and the oldest of six kids. His mom works down the street as a receptionist. Nathan is quite the football player but not quite the mathematician that I hear you are."

Raymond reached out his hand to shake Nathan's, but Nathan ignored it. "Nathan ... Nathan ..." Victor repeated until Nathan looked up at him. "This is Raymond. He is going to help you with your math every day for the next month. You might as well get used to him." Nathan acknowledged his presence and then looked back down at his desk.

Victor whispered, "He's a great kid. Give it some time." With that, he walked away as Raymond sat down.

"What did you do?" Nathan asked, as soon as Victor was out of range.

"What do you mean?" Raymond asked.

"I'm not stupid. Victor said you would be here for a month. Everyone who knows how long they're going to be here before they start is only here because they have to be. Usually, they got in trouble, so they spend time with us. So, what did you do?"

Raymond was flabbergasted at Nathan's boldness and wit. "I stole something," he said. Nathan just shook his head and kept working.

Raymond looked over Nathan's shoulder and observed his work. His math was atrocious. Raymond spent the next couple of minutes trying to figure out what to say next. "Nathan?"

"Yeah?" he huffed.

"You have to be here, right?"

"Yeah."

"You have to do your math homework, right?"

"Yeah, so what?" he said, raising his head in annoyance.

"Well, I have to be here too and I happen to be much better at math than stealing. So, how about I lend you my services for a month?"

 FAITH UNPLUGGED:

Those who love you prove their love by disciplining or correcting you when it's necessary.

Nathan pondered the offer and then accepted.

By the end of the first week, Nathan showed progress. Over the weekend, Raymond caught himself thinking and talking about Nathan. During the second week, Nathan continued to improve; Raymond began looking forward to the end of each school day. On Friday of the third week, Nathan completed an entire assignment without assistance or error. Nathan, upon hearing Raymond's evaluation, leaped from his seat and began to dance. Raymond laughed so hard that he snorted loudly, which briefly interrupted Nathan's groove. When he finally finished, Nathan hugged Raymond and whispered, "Thanks."

As his dad pulled the car away from the day care that night, Raymond saw Nathan waving the paper in front of his mom's face as they walked home. His mother beamed with pride. Raymond looked at his father and then said, "Dad, a couple of my friends' parents lied about their community-service hours to the judge or found them an easy way out. Thanks for making me do this. It really has changed me."

FAITH LINK:

Jesus, no one likes to be punished or disciplined, and I am no exception. I often wish I could just be let off the hook, but I know that even though it hurts, discipline changes me. Being held responsible for my actions develops my character and is a part of becoming the person you called me to be. Help me accept it with humility.

POWER UP:

Do you know anyone whose parents are always bailing him or her out? Do you know anyone who constantly avoids being held responsible for his or her actions? What kind of person do you think that person will become? Many people think that loving someone means forgiving consequence or that making a mistake in the first place is punishment enough. But love always does what is best for the other person. In this case, love disciplines because love desires that you will learn, grow, and mature. If your parents or friends continually bail you out, ask them to stop. When you allow yourself to be held accountable for your actions, you are making the determination to develop character in your life.

SPRING BREAK

Sacrifice

🐾📶 DOWNLOAD:

I'll make you a great nation and bless you. I'll make you famous; you'll be a blessing. Genesis 12:2

Tony Kirby ran for student government in the spring. He figured on an easy victory, and he was right. Most of the students in his San Diego high school liked him, and he won by a landslide. The newly elected student government met a few times at the end of the school year to brainstorm ideas for the following school year. One of the students, Abby Zachary, suggested that the school, or at least the student government, organize a trip to Tijuana for one of their breaks.

At first everyone thought it was an amazing idea, until Abby started talking about helping at an orphanage or building a home for a family. They, including Tony, were thinking about a week at the beach and cheap souvenirs. After a short debate, in which most of the students felt guilty for arguing in favor of relaxation and against helping others, the council voted to organize a service trip for spring break. Their adviser recommended that everyone in student government, pending parental permission, be required to go along with any willing students from the general population. After a long debate, they reluctantly agreed. It was much easier to approve the trip in theory than it was to vote in favor of sacrificing their own spring break to help others.

Throughout the summer and fall, no one, other than the volunteer organizers, Abby and Samantha, thought much about the trip. That was until January, when the advertising campaign began. The final plan was to take as many as sixty students to an orphanage for five days. There, they would spend their time helping not only with the children, but also with the construction of another home on the property. In the end, the trip would cost each student only three hundred dollars.

Tony's initial reaction was, *Who in their right mind is going to spend three hundred dollars to spend spring break at an orphanage? No way will we get sixty students to agree to that.* He was wrong.

Within the first three weeks, all sixty spots filled up, and the students paid in full. The response shocked Tony and delighted Abby and Samantha. He admitted that he'd misread the students' attitude toward this kind of thing.

Spring break came quickly and before they knew it, the students had gathered early at the school one Monday morning to load the buses.

"Students, may I have your attention please?" yelled Mr. Derrick, the school principal. "I want to thank you all for coming on this trip. I'm exceptionally proud of your commitment and sacrifice. I do want to talk to you briefly before we leave. I don't know how many of you have been to Tijuana before or how many of you have participated in a program similar to this. For those of you who have not, you need to prepare yourself to encounter some of the poorest living conditions in the world. What you see will surprise you, shock you, and break your heart. You can't fully imagine poverty until you have experienced it. If you have any questions or need to talk, please see me or one of the other chaperones."

"How bad can it be?" Tony asked, stirring a few nasty looks. "I didn't mean how bad could it be not having parents. I meant, how bad could the orphanage be?"

His explanation didn't ease the situation, so he decided to be quiet. Tony imagined the kids at the orphanage playing used Nintendo Gamecubes in a room similar to his family's den, only with used furniture and fewer decorations. Tony had never been on a trip like this one before, but he was confident everyone was overreacting and exaggerating as he laid his seat back to catch up on some sleep.

He awoke just on the other side of the border station. Rubbing his eyes, he looked outside to a street filled with beggars running up to the bus with empty coffee cans, vacant and desperate expressions, and tattered clothing. The site startled him so drastically that he could only stare. This was different from seeing a homeless man on the side of the street. He looked away, still expecting the orphanage to be quite different.

Thirty minutes and a zillion pot holes later, he discovered how naive he had been. Instead of four kids jovially playing a used Gamecube in

FAITH UNPLUGGED:

Love gives sacrificially.

the typical middle-class American living room downgraded with used furniture, he saw hundreds of kids in old clothes that they had probably worn for weeks, sitting outside on the grass scooping rice from a bowl with their bare hands. He could not believe his eyes, and the shock had only just begun.

The first two days contained one alarming discovery after another. He learned the old clothes were often the only clothes they owned. Hundreds of kids didn't mean hundreds of beds; most shared with two or three others. Rice was Monday's lunch, Monday's dinner, Tuesday's lunch, and Tuesday's dinner. The house they were building, which was only slightly bigger than Tony's bedroom, would become the home of eight orphans and a house mom. They had to boil the water, and the toilets were holes in the ground. Tony never knew people lived so differently than he did.

Tony's greatest discovery was compassion, which motivated him to work harder than he thought possible. He and the other students woke early to begin working. They worked through the afternoon heat and into the evening. After the sun set, they spent their nights playing with children and holding babies.

On Thursday night, the director of the orphanage met with their group after dinner. Tony sat in utter amazement at the director's attitude and service. After he finished talking, he took questions from the students. Tony raised his hand.

"Yes, Tony."

"I couldn't help but wonder all week, how much does it cost to keep a place like this running?"

"That's a great question, Tony. Thanks for asking that. I'm afraid the answer might surprise you."

"OK."

"It costs us somewhere between thirty and fifty dollars a month per child, which is probably close to what some of you spend over the course of an average weekend."

Back home, the director's answer felt like a cold slap to the face and echoed in his head as he stared around his room. Tony had just given up his spring break and three hundred dollars. He realized it was only a small sacrifice to make—but one that was making a big difference. He realized how much of his life he had spent consumed with himself. None of this stuff ever fulfilled him the way the past week had. He determined to live differently from that moment on, sacrificing his petty wants for others in need.

FAITH LINK:

Jesus, I have more than I need. Thank you for giving me so much. Help me become more like you and give in love, even when it is difficult. Take what you have given me and show me how to pass it on to those in need.

POWER UP:

Have you ever thought about how much you have to give? You can give not only your money and possessions, but also your time, talents, and skills. You have experiences to share and wisdom to pass on. God has given you so much and he intends for you to become a blessing to others. In doing so, you follow his example as the one who so loved us that he gave his only son. Furthermore, you will discover new meaning and significance in your life. Look for opportunities to generously give what has been given to you. Commit to live a sacrificial life just as Jesus did.

A TOWN CELEBRATION

Partying

Don't drink too much wine and get drunk; don't eat too much food and get fat. Drunks and gluttons will end up on skid row, in a stupor and dressed in rags. Proverbs 23:20–21

It was a Friday night in the fall, one of those Fridays students live for. The evening's football game pitted the hometown Cardinals against their archrival, the Eagles. The two teams would play for the district title and a slot in the state play-offs. This game called for a pep rally like no other. It lasted for nearly an hour. Highlighted by speeches from three players, the head cheerleader, the principal, and of course the head coach, this rally whipped everyone into frenzy. The hype lasted for another three hours, as everyone paused to eat and don their war gear.

A few hours later, just before they entered the locker room, one of the cheerleaders hailed three of the Cardinal players.

"Johnny, Blain, Tiny!" she said loud enough to grab their attention.

"Hey! What's up, Michelle?" Johnny responded, leading the others over to the fence nearby.

"Are you guys ready?"

"What kind of question is that?" Tiny asked. "We've been dreaming of this since we were kids."

"Good! Because when you win tonight, there's going to be a huge party out at the Hayes farm. I thought I'd let you know beforehand in case things get crazy after the game. So, spread the word. Everyone's invited." Michelle gave a quick wave and sprinted back to the rest of the squad.

"Boys, let's go win ourselves a ball game, and with any luck we'll be even luckier afterwards," Johnny exclaimed, throwing his arms over his teammates' shoulders. Blain and Tiny smiled knowingly as they headed into the locker room.

Fortunately, the game lived up to its hype. The Cardinals surged onto the field with the opening whistle and scored within the first three minutes. The Eagles fought back and by halftime had managed to pull ahead after halting the

FAITH UNPLUGGED:

The party scene is fun at first, but it will cost you something.

Cardinals' last drive and forcing them to settle for a field goal.

During halftime, both teams adjusted their defense, transforming the game into a near street fight for every yard. Both offenses showed signs of life, only to be squelched by some of the most fantastic defensive plays the fans had ever seen. The Cardinals, with a superior touchdown play by their senior quarterback, Blain, and wide receiver, Johnny, pulled ahead by three with just over a minute on the clock. A determined Cardinals defense shut down the Eagle offense, and the stands erupted.

Teenage girls screamed, moms wept, dads stood proudly shaking one another's hands and offering their congratulations to one another. Fans of all ages jumped the fence and ran onto the field in triumphant celebration, chanting, "On to state! On to state!" Players hoisted their helmets high in the air, lowering them only to hug a parent, teammate, coach, or fan. The band followed the celebrants onto the field, while playing the school fight song.

Two hours later, the celebration continued without waning at the Hayes farm. Students, players, cheerleaders, and band members yelled and screamed, danced and sang, drank and smoked, kissed and caressed. A surprising number of adults and alumni mingled in and around the student body.

Around one in the morning, Johnny, mildly toasted, and Michelle, slightly stoned, made their way to the car.

"Blain!" Michelle yelled, as Johnny dragged her along.

"What?" Blain yelled back.

"Who's that girl?" she asked, pointing to the person Blain was half carrying.

"I don't know."

"Bring her along!" Michelle shouted as Johnny shoved her into the front seat of the car. Blain picked up his girl and slung her over his shoulder.

Tiny, the only sober member of the group, noticed the scene and ran over. Laughingly he said, "Well, what do you kids think you're doing?"

"Tiny, I have to go home," slurred Michelle. "I have a curfew to keep so Daddy doesn't think I'm doing something bad." She went into a fit of uncontrollable laughter.

"Then who's driving this caravan?" Tiny asked with a smile.

"I am," replied Johnny with a belch, lifting himself off Michelle.

"You're in no condition to drive," Blain scolded, shaking his finger in Johnny's direction before falling straight back onto the ground.

Tiny pulled Blain up, forced him into the backseat, and grabbed the keys. "I think I'd better drive."

Fifteen minutes later, the car sat on the side of the road. Sirens roared nearby, and an officer approached the car. Michelle had puked as soon as they got on the highway, causing Tiny to swerve slightly. It was all the police needed to pull the car over.

On Monday morning, Johnny, Blain, Tiny, Michelle, and Juliana (the previously unnamed student) waited outside of the conference room as their parents and coach met with the principal. A few minutes later, the principal's secretary summoned them inside. Tiny received a one-game suspension from the team. If they won, he could return for the rest of the play-offs. That hope dimmed quickly as the other four students received a week suspension from school and a six-week suspension from all of their extracurricular activities.

Upon hearing the news, the town's morale sank to an unbelievable low. There would still be a pep rally on Friday, but everyone agreed the game was lost before the team had a chance to play.

 ## FAITH LINK:

Jesus, the party life is so alluring. All I see and hear are the entertaining aspects; very few ever talk about what it costs them in the end. Help me to resist the temptation to party and avoid the serious consequences that it inevitably causes. Give me a group of friends who do what is right and still have a blast.

 ## POWER UP:

Partying is glorified. It is painted in such an overwhelmingly positive light that you feel like you are missing out if you are not participating. What exactly are you missing? Fun and laughter? You don't have to party to have a good time. What you are really missing is a lot of drama complimented by headaches, vomiting, cheating, lying, backstabbing, casual sex, and potentially addictive illegal substances. If you are a part of the party scene, it is never too late to stop and walk away. Ask God to connect you with a different group of friends. If you are already a part of a close group of friends who are not caught up in the party life, thank God for them and let them know you appreciate them.

SPEAK UP

Friendship

DOWNLOAD:

Wounds from a friend can be trusted. Proverbs 27:6 NIV

Will and Simon knew their friendship wasn't the same as it once had been. These days, it required more work and attention. Both of them cared enough to put in the time, but both feared what a little strain might do. In turn, they avoided conflict whenever possible. They discovered that a casual, lighthearted friendship was much easier than the deep, committed one they had once shared. It became commonplace to avoid addressing certain topics or saying certain things. A morsel of their fourth-grade simplicity resided in their evasion and they liked it that way. They reminded each other of the good old days.

Last spring, Simon's life took an interesting turn that he kept hidden from his family and Will for as long as possible. He was waiting tables at a local restaurant, and he slowly joined "the scene." The restaurant scene involved all of the waitstaff converging on someone's apartment after closing to hang out. Due to his age, the other employees didn't invite Simon along at first. Simon, with his surprising amount of perceived maturity, quickly made friends and earned his way into the club. Club membership included certain "rights"—the right to drink, to smoke dope, to sleep over—or not to participate in any of the above. An unspoken rule held that whatever happened outside of work stayed outside of work, and the group extracted a promise from one another not to talk about the club to anyone who might bust it.

Simon exercised his right to nonparticipation. He didn't like the taste of alcohol. He believed smoking weed was stupid and dangerous, and he knew it was illegal. And if he slept over, his parents would make him quit his job. Still, Simon thoroughly enjoyed the company and laughter of his friends even when they were drunk or high. He went out with the waitstaff nearly every Friday night, and nearly every Friday someone offered him a chance to exercise his "rights."

One night, one of his lit-up coworkers decided to probe Simon's refusal to join in the fun. In particular he wanted to know why he wouldn't smoke pot.

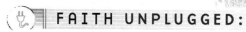

FAITH UNPLUGGED:

Your friends are those who will tell you the truth, even when it hurts.

"OK, Simon," Karl began. "Let me get this straight. You don't drink because you don't like it. You don't sleep over because you would get in trouble. You don't toke because ... why again?"

"No offense, but I think it's wrong."

"You think it's wrong, or you have bought the lies?"

Amused by his friend's animated question, he asked, "What's the difference?"

"Oh the difference is everything, my young friend. The difference is everything."

Over the course of the next hour, Simon listened to a persuasive speech on the benefits of marijuana usage, justification for legalizing marijuana, reasons behind the government's refusal to legalize it, and consequences it has on the American people and economy.

Simon spent most of the conversation doubled up on the couch completely entertained and astounded by the presence of persuasive logic in Karl's argument. It actually intrigued Simon enough to spend a little bit of his free time over the next couple weeks researching marijuana online.

A few Friday nights later, Simon had read enough pro-marijuana pitches to engage in another conversation with Karl. He had begun warming up to the idea, but he still had a few questions. After all, everything he read online and heard from his friend contradicted the opinions of his parents, school, church, and Will. After another hour-long conversation, he was ready to agree that weed use was definitely not as bad as he originally thought.

"Do you want to take a hit then?" Karl challenged.

"No, I'm still not using myself, but I agree with your stance and don't fault you for smoking," Simon responded, handing the joint back to his coworker.

"Suit yourself," Karl said, taking another hit. "That just leaves more for me."

Everyone in the circle laughed.

Over the next few weeks, Simon found himself in a surprising number of drug-related conversations. Either the topic came up more frequently, or for the first time Simon had something to offer to the discussion. One day at lunch, Simon and Will debated the issue briefly. Quickly recognizing that the subject might have a negative impact on their friendship, they moved to another topic. Will, however, walked away shocked and concerned about Simon.

Why was Simon so adamant about the benefits of lighting up? Will thought to himself. *He hasn't started getting high, has he? I wonder if I should ask him about it. On second thought, I probably should avoid that. I'm sure he's not.*

It didn't take long for Simon to move from marijuana advocate to consumer. He figured he would strengthen his argument with a few firsthand experiences. After all, knowledge can't make up for inexperience. The newfound understanding caused Simon to discuss the topic more freely. He even initiated a few arguments, including one with Will.

The discussion progressed like their first, but instead of stopping, they continued. Will noticed a slight change in Simon's language as well. He appeared to be speaking with an increased amount of passion and familiarity, which meant he became either more convinced through research or more resolute from an increased need to justify his consumption. Will listened to Simon rant while he debated whether to ask.

Asking will cause Simon to be offended or cause me to feel alarmed enough to do something before he gets himself in deeper trouble. What should I do? I'm his friend, so either I trust him and let him live his own life, or I act.

Simon's nonstop line of reasoning gave Will plenty of time to contemplate. He decided to ask. "Simon, can I ask you a question?"

"Sure, buddy!"

"Are you lighting up?"

Simon responded with an arrogance that surprised Will. "What do you think? Of course I am. I told you what I believe. I think we've been lied to our whole lives and denied one of life's simple pleasures."

"Simon, I hate to tell you this, but you're wrong."

Lord, prayed Will, *I've spoken the truth to Simon in love. I leave it in your hands now. Help me be available if he ever needs my help to stop what he's doing.*

 FAITH LINK:

Jesus, I need the kind of friends who will love me enough to speak up when I'm wrong. Help me to be open to what they have to say even when it's hard to hear. Give me the strength to speak up to my friends when I need to as well.

 POWER UP:

True friends are hard to find. Think about your friends for a minute. What kind of friends are they to you? What kind of friend are you to them? Are you open and honest with one another? Do you trust and love one another enough to say the things no one else is willing to say to each other? If so, that kind of friendship is rare and immeasurably important. Cherish those friends. If not, ask God to help your friendships transform or to bring new friends into your life. Finally, if one of your friends is getting involved in something that you know is wrong or dangerous, ask Jesus to help you say what could be the most difficult thing you have ever had to say.

TRUE ACTIVISTS

Citizenship

DOWNLOAD:

Obey your leaders and submit to their authority. They keep watch over you as men who must give an account. Obey them so that their work will be a joy, not a burden, for that would be of no advantage to you. Hebrews 13:17 NIV

"Can we stop talking about Iraq already? There are other issues involved in this election," Marissa voiced in frustration.

"All of the issues hinge on whether or not the person elected to the office of the president of the United States can be trusted. If that person attacks another country under false pretense, how can anyone be sure that anything he says is true?" Chad retorted.

It was always like this at lunch lately. Politics. Chad and Marissa argued while their two good friends, Monique and Mick, rolled their eyes or tried to play peacemaker. It would go on until the last tray was emptied in the trash can and they all made their way to their respective classes.

"Chad, I agree with you. Trust is essential, but there are people who trust him and people who don't," added Monique. "Arguing isn't going to change that. Marissa trusts him. You obviously don't. Let's move on."

"I'll try, but for the record I still think the fundamental issue is trust. Even though I'm open to discussing other issues, I do not trust anything he says in relationship to those issues. His approach might be right or better, but I cannot trust that he'll do what he says he will."

"We got it," Marissa huffed. Mick chuckled.

"Well, what should we fight about next?" Chad asked sarcastically, drawing an eye roll from Marissa.

"Taxes," suggested Mick with a sly smile.

"Mick, that's worse than talking about the war. It might actually create another one right here at our table, especially between these two," Monique added, pointing at Chad and Marissa.

"Taxes sound like an excellent topic. I'm actually curious to hear from Marissa how lowering the tax on America's wealthy actually helps the poor," Chad rejoined. "The idea has always fascinated me. Most fantasies do."

Mick and Monique fought to hold back their laughter.

"Chad, with your obviously superior intellect, you should know that helping the poor in our country involves much more than tax cuts. On the other hand, maybe you don't know that. I wonder if any of your kind does because it seems the only idea you ever have is to raise taxes. 'Raise taxes! Raise taxes! Raise taxes!'" Marissa shouted, pumping her fists in the air like a cheerleader.

Mick and Monique began crying as they continued to fight their giggles.

"Nice. Marissa, you have excellent form. I'm guessing from years of practice, listening to your candidates and chanting 'Whatever you say! Whatever you say! Whatever you say!'" Chad mocked. "In addition, I would like to point out that we have proposed much more tax-relief legislation related to the poor and disconnected than you ever have or will. Not to mention, we support a welfare-reform program that actually works."

Sensing that things might be getting a little too hot, Monique interrupted, "I told you not to bring up taxes or there will be bloodshed before the end of lunch."

"Are you afraid it will affect your appetite?" Mick joked, playing with the interesting concoction of food on his plate.

Everyone laughed, breaking the tension.

"You two are awfully quiet, well, apart from your obnoxious laughter," Marissa pointed out.

"I'm sorry. I didn't realize it was a 'discussion.' Are we also having 'discussions' in the Middle East?" Mick asked, making quotation-mark signs with his hands.

"Very funny, Mick," Chad acknowledged. "Seriously though, you're both moral people. What are your thoughts on poverty in the United States?"

Monique glanced at Mick and then responded. "We actually discussed this a few nights ago. I think I can speak for the both of us. We think both candidates have pretty good arguments, and we like parts of their plans. Rather than

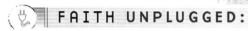 **FAITH UNPLUGGED:**

Criticism is not the same as activism.

choosing, wouldn't it be great if they could work together to create a strategy that would go beyond their party differences? I mean, a big reason for the constant debate and disagreement is that no party holds majority control long enough to get the ball rolling on long-term solutions before the other party takes over and rolls it the other way. I guess we're saying that the problem lies in the federal government. There is too much backbiting and finger-pointing happening in this country."

"Are you saying that the federal government is a hopeless cause, so you're not going to get involved?" Chad asked with a grin.

"Not at all," Mick replied. "I think we need to become more involved, but in a different way. Instead of jumping on the criticism bandwagon, we want to be a part of the solution."

"So what's your idea then?" asked Marissa.

"We want to vote for people who can work across party lines," Mick answered. "Hopefully officials will see the bigger picture, whether we voted for them or not. Then maybe we can have positive, solution-oriented conversations with each other."

Monique chimed in, "We're also going to start volunteering for the causes we believe in. Like this weekend, we're collecting nonperishable food items for one of the local food banks.

"Maybe we can make a difference in the fight against poverty without waiting on legislation," explained Mick.

"Well, aren't you just the model citizens?" Chad joked, half-impressed and slightly convicted.

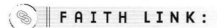

FAITH LINK:

Jesus, forgive me for pointing a finger at those you have placed in leadership in my life. Help me to speak positively and take positive actions toward change rather than criticizing from my couch.

POWER UP:

How many times have you heard someone criticize those in leadership or politics? Whom have you heard make the complaints? Do they know the whole story or are they making assumptions? What are they doing to help? What are you doing? You don't have to be an adult to make a difference in your community, state, or nation. A little initiative accompanied by a positive attitude and a willingness to serve can go a long way. God is looking for a new kind of activist—those who will volunteer their time and talents to help meet the needs around them. What are the needs in your community? What organizations or churches are working in that arena? Give them a call and get involved.

ARE YOU THREATENING ME?

Authority

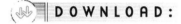

DOWNLOAD:

Submit yourselves for the Lord's sake to every authority instituted among men. 1 Peter 2:13 NIV

Trey chose subtle defiance over blatant rebellion. The strategy provided a sense of control without the consequences associated with direct disobedience. Granted, most of the adults in his life saw straight through his games, but they usually didn't possess enough evidence to enforce any discipline. Trey's friends knew the game and applauded his mastery.

In school, Trey pushed the limits farther than any of the other students did. He stepped into the classroom just long enough after the bell to avoid making a scene. Trey timed each teacher's turned back perfectly, allotting enough time to do as he pleased. In the halls, he stayed under the radar of the hall monitors with his rule breaking and pranks. He also played to each staff member's weakness. If a teacher displayed a propensity to allow talking in class, he exploited it. If another seemed lax in taking attendance, he carefully planned and skipped that class entirely. With regard to cutting class, he kept close tabs on his attendance in order to avoid suspicion while utilizing every allowed absence. He employed the same tactics with his homework.

At church, he walked a little over the line, taking advantage of his ability to manipulate those in leadership. If someone suggested Trey was manipulative, he just came back with a few well-timed comments about feeling judged and wanting to change, and they'd back off. Trey now only had to make subtle references to those conversations, and he could usually perform that nonverbally. It allowed him the freedom to get away with quite a bit—talking during the teaching, not participating in group activities, mocking others, and disappearing at will without consequence.

Trey played his games at home with his parents as well. His continually underhanded measures created space for the occasionally more deliberate revolt, and he took advantage of this. He knew he straddled a dangerous line between intimidating his parents and pushing them over the edge. The potential costs of crossing the line at home were much greater than crossing them at church or school. On the other hand, gaining control at home provided a much greater benefit than anywhere else. Walking the line took an enormous amount of energy, and it was becoming more difficult.

Saturday morning around ten o'clock, his mom woke him up.

"What time is it?"

"It's ten o'clock. It's time for you to get out of bed," she politely ordered.

"No, it's too early. Turn the light off, so I can go back to sleep."

"Early? What time did you come home last night?" she inquired.

"Late," he said curtly.

"Trey," she said more firmly, "how late is 'late'?"

"I don't remember. Now turn the light off and let me sleep," he moaned in frustration and avoidance.

"Trey William Scott," his mom asked sternly, "what time did you come home?"

Trey sat straight up, looked his mom in the eye, suddenly much more awake, and said bluntly, "Mom, I told you I don't remember.

Now turn the light off and if you still want to talk about this when I wake up, we will. Good-bye."

His mom was really not shocked at the clarity and force with which Trey spoke. She stood quietly and walked out of the room to discuss the matter with her husband.

A few hours later, Trey rolled out of bed and into the kitchen for food. His parents sat at the counter waiting. His dad spoke first.

"Son, we need to talk."

"Ahhh, Dad," he said sympathetically, "if this is about what happened this morning, I'm sorry." He turned to his mother while pouring a bowl of cereal. "Mom, I'm sorry. You know what I'm like in the morning. I say things that I don't mean when I'm tired. It was early, and I was tired. I didn't mean to be rude. I'm sorry."

 **FAITH UNPLUGGED:**

Most people's problems with authority lie within themselves rather than with the authority.

"Being tired is no excuse to talk to your mother that way."

"Dad, I said I'm sorry. I'll work on not being so cranky in the morning, but I can't make any promises. I can't help the way that I am." He finished by taking a big bite of cereal, downplaying the seriousness of the conversation.

"Son, this is not a joke."

With a mouthful of Fruity Pebbles, he mumbled, "Dad, I never said it was a joke. I apologized, and that's the end of the conversation. Now, I'm hungry and want to eat."

"I'll decide when this conversation is over, not you," his dad fumed.

Trey realized he'd pushed too hard and attempted to recover the situation. "I'm sorry, Dad. You know I didn't mean that in a bad way. I'm just hungry. I'm sorry I came across like I was joking or downplaying the situation." Turning back to his mom, he repeated, "Mom, I really am sorry for being short with you this morning. I didn't mean to yell at you or order you around. Please forgive me."

"Trey, I forgive you, but this is a much bigger matter than this morning."

Playing naive to keep the conversation under control, Trey asked, "What do you mean?"

"Trey, you know exactly what we're talking about," his dad replied more firmly.

Trey recognized the need to backpedal further. He lowered his head and began, "I know, and I really am sorry. I haven't been very pleasant to be around lately. I guess school and stuff is really stressing me out. Sorry I'm taking it out on you."

"Trey, this isn't just about us or you feeling stressed. This is a problem," added his dad, causing Trey to sweat while looking for his next move.

"We received a call yesterday from one of your teachers," his mom rejoined.

"Why? I haven't done anything wrong," announced Trey, confident and perturbed. "Who called?"

"Mrs. McMichael," his mom responded.

"The principal?" Trey asked, faking surprise.

"It turns out that quite a few teachers brought up your name during the staff in-service day," his dad pronounced.

"Those teachers hate me. They've all been out to get me since day one. I never did anything to them, and they treat me like this."

"Son, I hate to say this, but the sympathy card isn't going to work this time. If this involved one or two teachers, maybe, but all your teachers are saying the same thing. I don't think you're the victim here. Your mother and I agree that you have a problem with authority."

"You're taking their side then?"

"Trey, we aren't taking sides," his mother firmly stated.

"Whatever!" Trey yelled. "Of course you're taking their side because then it's my problem and not yours!"

"Trey, settle down," his mother requested.

"No! This is ridiculous. I don't have to take this from you or anyone else. If I have a problem with authority, it's because of you and those idiots at school. I'm not listening to this. This is not my problem." Trey turned and began to leave the room.

"Trey," his father's voice boomed. "Get back here and sit down or there will be serious consequences."

"Are you threatening me?"

"Yes, I am."

Trey had never seen his parents like this before. Maybe after all these years, he had finally pushed them over the edge. He didn't know how he was going to get out of this one. Maybe he could pretend to give in and then manipulate his way out later. He began spinning ideas in his head.

Meanwhile, his father continued, "I'm not saying that we aren't partially to blame. I'm afraid that your mother and I allowed you to get away with too much, but that doesn't release you from accountability. You have gone too far, and it's our job to bring you back. You might hate us even more after this, but we're willing to take that risk. Submitting to authority, whether you like the people in the position or not, is a big part of life and adulthood. Things are going to change around here, at school, and at church. We love you enough to try to stop this before you or someone else ends up getting hurt. If you don't think that will happen, let me take you down to the prison and you can see it firsthand."

 ## FAITH LINK:

Jesus, you placed these people in a position of authority in my life. Truthfully, I'm having a difficult time accepting their place and role. I don't want or think I need them, yet you think I do. I know your perspective is better than mine, so help me to trust you. In doing so, help me submit to them.

POWER UP:

As a teenager, you're caught in the strange place between complete dependence on the adults in your life and establishing your own independence. Most teens want to speed the process up as quickly as possible and think that life will be better and easier when they're on their own. The truth is you are never on your own. There will also be people who are in authority over you. When you go to college, you will have professors, administrators, resident advisors, etc. Also, you'll have a landlord, boss, and the government. Of course, there will always be God, who is the highest authority. Authority is not a bad thing. In fact, it was God's idea in the first place, and it works really well when everyone plays his or her part. Usually the trouble falls with those under authority, not the people in authority themselves. If you are struggling with authority, ask God to help you. He has placed those people in your life to help and challenge you to grow. Resisting them is resisting God. Occasionally, you might be in a situation where someone is abusing the authority they have been given. You might even be in that situation now. If so, trust that the God of justice is moving on your behalf and continue to submit as best you can without violating your values.

THE HARDEST ONE

Forgiveness

On the other hand, if we admit our sins—make a clean breast of them—he won't let us down; he'll be true to himself. He'll forgive our sins and purge us of all wrongdoing.   1 John 1:9

"I'm sorry," Brad said. He said it all the time, even when he didn't need to say it. This time he told his teacher when he answered a question incorrectly. The time before, he had drifted off slightly in class. Another time he apologized for being confused and needing a little extra help.

"Excuse me. Sorry. Excuse me," Brad whispered as he walked down the hall with his head lowered and his eyes peering out. The same thing happened at the mall and at church.

"OK, sorry," he told his boss after he asked him to do something. He should have just known, right? Those words followed numerous conversations with his boss at the car wash, team leaders, coworkers, and even customers.

"So sorry, guys." Brad spoke these words to his friends consistently. He was sorry for being early, sorry for being late, and sorry for being on time. He apologized for speaking and for not saying a thing. Brad asked for forgiveness when he thought he was annoying them and for when his asking became annoying. Most of the time, he tried not to say or do too much. It was better to be safe than sorry. He didn't want to drive them away.

"Sorry, Mom, please forgive me," Brad requested when his mom asked him how much longer he would be on the phone. "No problem, honey. I just need to use it when you're done, but it's no rush." Brad hung up.

Brad appealed to his mom when it took him a little longer to get ready for school one morning. "Honey, it's no problem," she said, "we have plenty of time." Then Brad apologized for apologizing. He repeated the phrase when they hit all the stop-lights on the way.

When he needed to call his mom at work for anything at all, he would say it again. "Brad, it's OK for you to call me at work. You know that."

"You're right, Mom, sorry."

"Dad, I'm sorry," he stated even more frequently. He spoke those words every time they talked on the phone or saw each other in person. He said them when he felt he called too often or not enough. Brad uttered them when he could not do something because of prior plans. (Sometimes he would cancel the other arrangements and apologize to those people.) He verbalized them when his father asked him a question about something he thought he should have already told him.

The only other things he said as often as "sorry" were self-directed demeaning remarks. "I'm not very good at math. I'm so stupid. I'm always getting in the way. I'm such a klutz. I have to be the most annoying person. I don't mean to be a burden. I'm not good at anything. I look horrible. I hate it when I do that."

One Friday night, his mom sat in her favorite chair reading a book when Brad came downstairs. He saw his mom was reading and apologized for being too loud.

"You weren't loud at all."

"OK then. Sorry to interrupt then." Brad responded as he walked out of the living room and into the kitchen.

His mom shouted after him, "Brad, what are you doing tonight? Are you going out with your friends?"

Brad yelled back, "Sorry, I forgot to tell you. I don't have any plans, so I was just going to stay here tonight. Is that OK?" he asked while walking back into the living room.

"Of course it's OK. I love having you home with me. You've been spending a lot of time at home recently. Is everything OK with your friends?"

"Yeah," he said quietly, "everything is great. I haven't been doing a lot with them on the weekends because I don't want to mess up their plans. Sorry that I've been home so much. I hope I haven't been getting in your way."

"Brad," his mom responded sympathetically, "you never get in my way. Come over here. Let's talk." She moved over on the love seat so there was plenty of room for both of them. "What's really going on?"

FAITH UNPLUGGED:

Sometimes the hardest person to forgive is yourself.

"Nothing, Mom," Brad answered. "Honestly, everything is pretty good."

"Brad, you just haven't been yourself lately. I've been worried about you."

"I'm sorry, Mom. I didn't mean to make you worried."

"Honey, it's OK for me to worry about you. I love you, and I'm your mother."

"OK," Brad responded hesitantly, and then before he could stop himself he added, "Sorry."

"This is what I'm talking about, Brad. You seem to be really down on yourself, and you apologize all the time. Most of the time it's for no real reason. It feels like you're apologizing for just being you."

Silence filled the room as Brad looked away from his mom. He wanted to apologize, but knew he couldn't after his mom's statement. The two sat quietly for a few minutes, before Brad's mom spoke again.

"Why do you feel like you need to ask for forgiveness or put yourself down all the time? I don't understand. You are an amazing young man who makes me so proud."

Tears welled in Brad's eyes, and he hung his head, unable to look up at his mom.

"Brad, talk to me, please."

"Mom, I'm so sorry. I'm so sorry. I didn't mean to. I promise. I didn't mean to. Please forgive me, I'm so sorry," he cried.

"Brad, what are you sorry for?" his mom asked.

Brad looked up briefly and said, "I'm sorry for making Dad leave." He tried to hold back a sob.

His mom wiped her eyes before responding. "Brad, your father didn't leave because of you. Our divorce happened for many reasons, but you most assuredly were not one of them. In fact, if it hadn't been for you, we probably wouldn't be speaking to each other. Brad, you hold us together, not pull us apart. Have you blamed yourself this entire time?"

"I just thought it was my fault. I never knew the reasons. I guessed you and Dad didn't want to tell me because you didn't want to hurt me."

"No, Brad, we didn't tell you because we didn't want anything to separate either one of us from you. Does that make sense?"

"It makes sense, but it doesn't change how I feel. I still feel guilty."

"Brad, we all experience feelings of guilt sometimes. Sometimes for things we have done; other times for things that aren't our fault. One of the hardest parts of life is learning how to forgive yourself. Whether you're to blame or not doesn't matter; you're still worth forgiving. That process begins with seeing yourself in the right light. Right now, you believe many things about yourself that are not true. It might take some time to change that, but tonight would be a great time to begin."

FAITH LINK:

Jesus, I'm living with guilt, shame, and regret. I have a hard time forgiving myself. I feel like I need to punish myself or somehow earn forgiveness, but no matter what I do, it doesn't take the feelings away. I need help allowing your forgiveness to be enough for me. I open up and ask that you help me to forgive myself.

POWER UP:

As difficult as it is to forgive others, it's sometimes more difficult to forgive yourself. Do you continually feel guilty or ashamed for something that happened a long time ago? Do you feel guilty about the same thing all the time? Jesus came, lived, died, and rose from the grave to bring you into a full and free life, not one controlled by guilt. Forgiving yourself might not be easy, but you need to be willing to start. If not, you are saying that Jesus' sacrifice wasn't enough to pay for your mistakes. Let Jesus be enough for you. Yes, you should admit your mistakes and take responsibility for them. But take them to Jesus, learn from them, and allow his forgiveness to overwhelm you.

INDIA AND THE TABLE

Love

DOWNLOAD:

If anyone boasts, "I love God," and goes right on hating his
brother or sister, thinking nothing of it, he is a liar. If he won't
love the person he can see, how can he love the God he can't see?
1 John 4:20

Malcolm was watching his favorite television show at the
time of the interruption.

"We interrupt this regularly scheduled broadcast to bring
you this special report."

"No!" shouted Malcolm. "It was just getting interesting."

The station switched from his show to a location in
Southeast Asia where a newscaster was standing by.

"Good evening, America. This is Michelle Blake with *NBC
News*...."

Malcolm looked desperately for the remote control, ignoring
the special report. As he aimed the remote toward the television, he stopped short at the images on the screen. The camera
panned over a bewildered mother holding her screaming child,
a man sitting with his face buried in his hands, and a child
standing alone, looking aimlessly around, too afraid to cry.

The camera panned over a vast landscape of disaster. The scene from above looked eerily peaceful. Smoke drifted gently in a sunset-streaked sky.

Malcolm refocused on the newscaster's voice.

"This is one of the worst earthquakes in recorded history. It measured 8.7 on the Richter scale, but that number does not translate into the numbers of lives lost and families left without homes. The earthquake occurred approximately thirty minutes ago, so it's too early to assess the damages accurately. As you can tell from the footage, I think it's safe to estimate deaths in the thousands. What we have to remember is that each one of those potential deaths represents someone's husband or wife, mother or father, brother or sister, friend or relative. In addition, an earthquake of this magnitude will cause numerous aftershocks afflicting even more damage and taking more lives. We will keep you updated as this story progresses. This is Michelle Blake for *NBC News*."

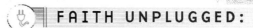

FAITH UNPLUGGED:

The hardest people to love are often the people you love the most.

"Now back to your regularly scheduled program."

The television cut back to a show that now seemed quite trivial to Malcolm. The image of the lone child standing in the middle of the street surrounded by rubble, covered in dirt, and terrified flashed continually before his eyes. He felt compassion for a nameless stranger, something he never felt before. At the same time, he felt unattached and unable to do anything to ease the child's suffering and pain.

Forty-five minutes earlier, Malcolm had eaten dinner with his parents and his younger siblings. Malcolm's younger brother, Andre, was only two years younger. His sister, Toni, was the baby in the family at eight years old. Family dinners were always interesting. Malcolm's parents, Steve and Andrea, spent most dinners resolving the continual sibling conflicts. The most intense fighting revolved around Malcolm and Andre.

From an outside perspective, the two brothers hated each other. They rarely spoke to each other unless they were angry. Malcolm found Andre incredibly irritating, self-righteous, and too dependent on their parents for everything. Andre thought of Malcolm as selfish, prideful, and ungrateful.

"So, Malcolm, how was your day?" his father asked.

"It was fine," Malcolm said tersely.

"Don't snap at Dad like that," Andre rebuked.

"I didn't snap at Dad, and don't tell me what to do," Malcolm snapped back.

"Boys!" their mother exclaimed.

"I'm sorry, Mom. I'm just sick of the way he treats you and Dad," Andre responded.

"Just because I'm not sucking up doesn't mean that I treat them badly," Malcolm shouted at his brother. "I'm sick of you pointing fingers at me trying to make yourself look good. What are you after anyway? If you're fighting for the favorite-child spot, you can have it."

"Andre, Malcolm, stop it, please," their father rejoined harshly. "Your mother and I are getting tired of both of your nitpicking at one another. I don't understand why it's seemingly impossible for you to be in the same room together without hatred spilling all over the place. You are family for goodness sake. The way you treat each other is shameful."

The boys finished their dinner in silence, looking only at their plates and spending more time playing with their food than eating it. Toni took advantage of her parents' undivided attention to brag about herself. They listened halfheartedly, upset by the conflict and agitated by Toni's lack of sensitivity and endless chatter.

"May I be excused?" Malcolm asked.

"Go ahead," his dad responded.

He rinsed his plate, placed it in the dishwasher, and headed for the living room. Andre followed about three minutes behind. They both had made plans to watch different television shows without telling the other. When Andre reached the living room, he saw Malcolm on the couch, remote in hand.

"Turn it to channel six," Andre ordered.

"Excuse me?" Malcolm retorted.

"Channel six!" Andre shouted slowly and deliberately, as if Malcolm couldn't understand.

"Sorry, stupid. I'm watching channel two tonight," Malcolm shot back.

"You had the TV last night. I get it tonight."

"The TV is first come, first serve, and I was here first. If you want to run along and cry to Mommy and Daddy, I'm sure they would love it after the display you put on at dinner."

"You are such a jerk," Andre said, fighting to keep his voice down.

"Just shut up already. I get it, Andre," Malcolm roared. "You are the sweet, innocent, perfect child, and I'm the ungrateful jerk that you got stuck with as your older brother. The one thing that you might not understand is that I loved my life until you came along with your holier-than-thou but surprisingly hypocritical brother act. I don't buy it and neither do Mom and Dad. Give it up and get out of my face!"

Andre shot a look Malcolm's way, turned, and walked upstairs to his room.

Forty-five minutes later, Malcolm's father sat down next to him on the couch. A tear rolled down Malcolm's cheek. "Malcolm, what's wrong?" his father gently asked.

"An earthquake struck India a few minutes ago. They just showed some of the footage on TV. It was total chaos. People were running and screaming everywhere. Then they showed a little boy standing alone in the street. I haven't been able to stop thinking about him. He looked so helpless. I wish there was something I could do."

"Malcolm, there are things you can do. You can start by praying, and I'm sure in the next few days there will be plenty of chances to give. It might not seem like much, but it's a start."

"I guess you're right."

"I'm proud of you for having the right idea, Malcolm. If you really want to show someone you love him, your actions have to show it. Love is meaningless without action to back it up."

As his dad was talking, Malcolm began to realize that he was talking about more than just the tragedy in India. He was also referring to the tragedy happening at home between two brothers.

FAITH LINK:

Jesus, it's amazing to me that I can find myself loving you, my invisible God, strangers, and people around the world. Thank you for filling my heart with your compassion. At the same time, it can be hard for me to demonstrate your love to my family, close friends, classmates, coworkers, teammates, coaches, teachers, and neighbors. Help me to love them the same way that you love me.

POWER UP:

Our culture tells us that love is a feeling or emotion. Though at times we can feel love, that is not essentially what it is. Love is a decision to act in a certain way toward another person. It is being patient, kind, humble, selfless, forgiving, and encouraging. It's the action of protecting, trusting, and remaining hopeful to those around you. How are you doing at loving those around you? Think about the people in your life. Are you treating them in this manner? Why or why not? If not, start today. Talk to those people and ask for their forgiveness. Commit to act in love toward them. Ask them how you can best demonstrate love toward them. This will give you some practical ideas and suggestions to start. Continue to ask God to teach you and fill you with his love.

WILLIE'S RED RIBBON

Service

DOWNLOAD:

That is what the Son of Man has done: He came to serve, not be served—and then to give away his life in exchange for the many who are held hostage. Matthew 20:28

Jamie reached his breaking point sometime in March. It had been a horrible year of compounded frustration and confusion. His girlfriend flew south for the summer and returned north with a new boyfriend. In the fall, his studies drifted, and his grades followed. Over Christmas break, things grew tense between his parents. By March, they announced a temporary separation while they sought counseling. Jamie, in turn, decided it was time to throw in the towel, give up for the year, and hope next year would be better. Until then, he focused on sorting through his thoughts, attempting to figure out his life and all that had happened.

"Good morning, class," Mr. Kennedy greeted his first-hour Monday world history students. "I hope everyone had a great weekend." The students muttered under their breath in response. "Before we dive into today's lesson about the catalysts for World War II, I want to talk to you about a volunteer opportunity."

Jamie and half the class tried unsuccessfully to tune Mr. Kennedy out. They were instinctively wary of the phrase "volunteer opportunity." But they found it hard to resist his passion and enthusiasm.

"For the last three years, I've had the privilege of coordinating volunteers to assist with the Special Olympics. Each year I ask students from my classes to help with the athletes by being their friends. Friends hang out with the athletes, monitor and encourage them, and make sure they get to their events on time. If you're interested, please sign your name on the sheet that I will pass around during class. Any questions?" In response, he was greeted by a classroom full of blank, glazed stares.

"OK. Let's talk about World War II then."

When the bell rang, a majority of the class, suddenly very awake, sprinted out the door.

Jamie, lacking the energy or motivation to run, lagged behind. Mr. Kennedy glanced at the sign-up sheet and noticed Jamie hadn't volunteered. Jamie knew Mr. Kennedy well. Mr. K had taught his two older siblings and was a longtime family friend. With his history with Jamie and knowledge of the current situation, he thought he would ask him about it.

"Jamie. Can I talk to you for a second?"

"Sure," he mumbled, turning toward his desk.

"I noticed that you didn't sign up to help with the Special Olympics."

"Mr. K, I just can't handle anything like that right now. There's just too much stuff going on in my head. You know that," he stated, irritated at having to justify himself to someone who already knew what he was going through.

"Jamie, I know you've got a lot on your plate right now. That is actually why I mentioned it. I think something like this would be therapeutic and, believe it or not, quite enjoyable. I don't need an answer today. Just do me a favor and think about it. OK?"

"Sure thing," he muttered, relieved that the conversation was over. He turned and walked out the door.

Mr. K said nothing about the Special Olympics to Jamie on Tuesday, but he cornered him after class on Wednesday.

"Well, Jamie, did you give it some thought?" he asked.

"I did, Mr. K. I just can't do it right now. I'm sorry."

"It's no problem, Jamie. How about I give you a few more days to think about it, and I'll ask you again on Friday?" he pestered.

"Mr. Kennedy, are you going to keep asking me until I say yes?" he asked, annoyed but also a little amused.

"That's my plan!" he said, smiling. "I know you don't want to do this. I guess I'm asking you to trust me on this one. Just give it a shot. I think you'll love it. If I'm wrong, then I'll never ask you to do anything again."

"All right, I'll do it," he conceded, "but only to get you to stop bugging me." He faintly smiled and walked out of the room.

Two weeks later on a Saturday, Jamie reported to the high school track at eight o'clock in the morning. Mr. Kennedy spotted him while giving instructions to a large group of volunteers. He motioned for him to wait there for one minute. Jamie looked around. The number of volunteers impressed him as he waved to a classmate across the way.

"Hey, Jamie, it's good to see you!" exclaimed a bright-eyed Mr. Kennedy.

"You too," Jamie replied quietly.

"Let me introduce you to your friend. His name is Willie. He is fifty-six years old, fast as lightning, and a little girl crazy so watch out." Mr. Kennedy's comment coaxed a smile on Jamie's face as they walked onto the track to meet Willie.

"Willie! Willie!" Mr. K shouted to a somewhat hunchbacked, balding, middle-aged man. Willie sprinted over. "Willie, I want to introduce you to Jamie. He will be your friend today."

"Hi, Jamie. Hi, I'm Willie, and I'm going to win the race. Yeah, I'm going to win," Willie stated with a confident smile, a few twitches, and a firm handshake.

"Jamie, Willie is competing in the hundred-yard dash at eleven and the shot put at twelve forty-five. Can you make sure he gets there and stays there to receive his ribbon if he wins?"

"Yeah, I'm going to win!" Willie added.

"Sure thing, Mr. K," Jamie rejoined with another smile and a tiny chuckle.

Mr. K turned around and Willie immediately took off running across the field. Jamie hesitated and then ran after him. *I guess this is his warm-up,* he thought. For the next few hours, Jamie spent most of his time running to catch up with Willie. Willie only stopped to show an occasional magic trick, which he found quite entertaining, or to talk to a pretty girl. Luckily, Willie thought every girl was pretty. He quit running often, allowing Jamie time to catch up and catch his breath.

 FAITH UNPLUGGED:

When you feel stuck, don't look inside yourself for answers. Look around for opportunities to serve and give a part of yourself to the success of someone else. Life begins to sing when you help others.

Three hours ticked by so fast, he nearly missed taking Willie to the 100-yard dash. It was a good thing they didn't miss it. Even though he had run all morning, Willie had enough steam to win his heat and clock the second-fastest time overall. Jamie had never witnessed this level of excitement.

"I'm going to win. I'm going to win. I get a ribbon. Yeah, I get a ribbon. Second place. Second place. Second place!" Willie yelled when he heard the news. He was so exuberant; he took off running to tell all of his new friends. Jamie chased him down before he got too far ahead of him.

"Willie, we have to go back and get your ribbon first. Then we can show everyone," he stated persuasively, as the look in Willie's eye told him he could run at any minute.

"Yeah, I get a ribbon. I get a ribbon. What color?"

"Red, I think," Jamie said, smiling ear to ear.

"I like red. I get a red ribbon. Then we will show my friends my red ribbon," Willie agreed. He grabbed Jamie's hand and led a team jog back to the finish line.

A few hours, thirty-nine laps around the field, and a third-place finish in the shot put later, Willie boarded his bus to go home. Exhausted, Jamie sat on the curb waving good-bye. He was unaware that Mr. K stood right behind him.

"I told you," he said.

He turned around to see Mr. K grinning. He was now smiling ear to ear. He continued, "Sometimes the best way to sort through life is not to look inside at ourselves, but outside to others. Thanks for your help, Jamie. See you on Monday."

Mr. K walked away as Jamie turned back around to see Willie's head and arm hanging out the window of the bus. He clutched his ribbons, waved, and yelled, "I'm going to win!"

FAITH LINK:

Jesus, you blow my mind. You entered your creation not to be served by it, but to serve it in the most radical way possible. You gave your life away. Help me to do the same thing. Help me to give my life to others and use my simple actions to advance your purposes in the world.

POWER UP:

Have you ever felt depressed? Have you ever felt confused or frustrated? What did you do during those times? When life becomes difficult, many people turn inward to try to figure things out. They become isolated and introspective. They determine that the best way through the mess is to focus on their problems. Unfortunately, when you do that, your problems often appear larger and insurmountable. Jesus taught a different model. Put others first. In your sorrow, depression, confusion, and frustration, serve others. Amazingly, life comes into focus when you do this. The problems that seemed large and impossible suddenly become manageable and even solvable. Look for chances to serve others, and see how your life changes.

BLACK DOG ON A GRAVEL ROAD

Responsibility

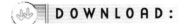

DOWNLOAD:

Each of you must take responsibility for doing the creative best you can with your own life. Galatians 6:5

At last glance the black 2003 Honda Civic's speedometer read eighty-five miles per hour. Jamin might have been going faster, but he was paying closer attention to the clock than his speed. His mom wanted him home twenty minutes ago, but spending the day at his friend Olivia's house frequently caused Jamin to lose track of time. He would rather be with her family than anywhere else.

Olivia's family lived on a farm about ten minutes outside of town. Her parents, Larry and Joy, treated him like the son they never had. Jamin and Olivia had been friends since the sixth grade. Granted, he often wished they dated, but their friendship became more like family, especially after this last year. They both went through quite a lot of drama as sophomores and leaned heavily on each other. Hanging out all day on Saturdays was quite normal for the two of them.

This Saturday, like most, Jamin woke around nine thirty and raced to Olivia's house by ten. Joy had some fresh-baked goodies waiting for him. By ten, Larry had been working for a couple of hours already. Jamin often honked at him while driving up the quarter-mile driveway. Jamin and Joy exchanged their common conversation about family, school, extracurricular activities, and the potential of any budding female relationships. Joy asked about the latter, always hoping such a relationship would one day include her daughter. This often led to their conversations ending in an awkward pause complemented by Jamin shoving another muffin or cookie in his mouth.

"So, let me guess," Jamin said, breaking the silence, "she's asleep upstairs."

"I'm sure she's waiting for you to wake her up."

"Thanks, Mom. I'll see you in a little bit," Jamin responded as he bounded up the stairs. He had been calling Olivia's parents "Mom" and "Dad" for years. Joy loved it.

"Olivia! Get your lazy rear out of bed," he yelled as he reached her door. Olivia never responded to his yell, but his elbow drop usually worked. He dropped his elbow on her side. "Wakey, wakey, Sis!"

Sleepily, Olivia said, "Hey, Bro, how are you?"

"I'm good. You?"

"I would be better if you got off me," Olivia grunted, attempting to push Jamin onto the floor. He had already braced himself for her inevitable try.

"That was better this week. Have you been working out?" he mocked.

"Get out of my room," she said, pushing him again.

"That's a little overreactive, don't you think?" he said with a laugh, knowing it was time for her to get ready for the day. He stepped out of her room to give her some privacy.

A few minutes later, Olivia called him back in. They spent the next couple of hours talking, while periodically making fun of each other, and eventually delving into the deeper portions of their souls. All of that before lunch, no less. Lunch called Jamin's stomach around one o'clock. It usually spoke through Joy's gentle hog call.

"Olivia! Jamin! Lunch is ready!"

The moment the words reached his ears, Jamin's conversational abilities decreased instantaneously, and he rushed downstairs to the table. It was the combination of home cooking and Larry's presence that drew Jamin to the table. Meals never lasted long enough. There were always more chores for Larry to finish.

That afternoon, Jamin and Olivia repeated much of the morning. They talked. They laughed. Then they watched a DVD. Olivia usually recommended watching a movie because Jamin spoke more honestly and openly afterwards. It was the openness and the honesty that made him run late that day.

"Oh no," Jamin yelped in the middle of a sentence.

"What's wrong?" Olivia asked.

"I'm late. I told my mom I would be home by six for dinner. I gotta run. She told me if I was late again, she was taking my baby away for a week."

"By your baby, you mean your car, right?"

"Right," he stated, jumping up off the couch.

"Well, it's a good thing you drive fast," joked Olivia as Jamin ran out the door.

He jumped in his car and took off down the driveway. He decided to take the shortcut down a gravel road to shave a few minutes off his time. The normal lack of police officers on the back roads didn't hurt his cause. In addition, Jamin never avoided an opportunity to put his car to the test. He had taken this road a few hundred times to and from Olivia's house. In fact, he had used the same road earlier that day.

Within the first few minutes, the car reached eighty-five. Twenty seconds later he screamed over the top of a small hill about two miles down the road. He hadn't noticed the new gravel on this side of the road on his way to Olivia's. Jamin was going too fast and not paying close enough attention when he hit the loose gravel straight on.

He felt the car shift to the right on the rocks then back to the left. Panicked, he slammed on the brakes, making the problem even worse. The brakes, unable to slow the skid, locked up, causing his Civic to spin out of control.

The car spun completely around. Then it spun repeatedly. Three and a half doughnuts in all before the car, pointing in the opposite direction, slid into the ditch and turned on its side. Jamin was terrified. He had frozen during the first spin, forgetting any countermeasures he could have taken. The car rested on the passenger side. He opened his door and crawled out, shaking but unharmed. A little sore, of course, but it could have been worse. He could have been in the same shape as his car. It wasn't totaled, but Jamin's baby looked rough.

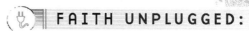

FAITH UNPLUGGED:

Taking responsibility for the way you live is the best response to God's ability to bring good into everything.

Jamin looked around and saw that the closest farmhouse was a quarter of a mile away. During his walk of shame, he attempted to concoct different scenarios that would explain the accident. *The loose gravel might be able to stand alone, especially if it was at the base of the hill. I just didn't see it. I could try to include another car in the story, like I swerved and lost control because of some other driver's lack of concern. I wonder if the police would investigate something like that? It's probably best not to try. Of course, I could also blame it on an animal. I'm in the country, and someone around here has to own a black dog.*

As he neared the house, Jamin rehearsed his speech. "Mom, before I say anything else, I want you to know that I'm OK. Secondly, it's not my fault. Now let me explain what happened...." He felt pleased with the amount of progress he made in such a short amount of time. *I wonder if I pull off the animal excuse, will I have to pay for the damages?*

Kindly, the residents of the closest farmhouse let Jamin use their phone to call his mom. He didn't know exactly what happened to his cell phone during the accident. Jamin's mom answered. He delivered the speech perfectly, and she was on her way.

As he waited, the local farmer stood outside waiting with him.

"Black dog, huh?" he asked, then turned and walked inside.

Jamin said nothing. He suddenly realized how ridiculous and wrong his fairy tale really was. The reality of the situation was that it was his fault and his alone. He needed to accept the responsibility for that no matter what the consequences. Fearing the loss of his license, the cost of the repairs or the insurance increase, or the loss of his car altogether, he decided taking responsibility, though costly, weighed better on his conscience.

FAITH LINK:

Jesus, avoiding responsibility for my words and actions seems so simple and easy, which makes it so inviting. Nevertheless, you instruct me to follow your example. No one took more responsibility for his life than you did. Give me the grace and strength to do the same, trusting that in doing so you will be with me when it's difficult. I know you're working with me even when I can't see you.

POWER UP:

Have you ever thought about how the world around you treats responsibility? What is the impression you get from TV, music, movies, professional sports, and even sometimes those in leadership? Do you see people denying responsibility? Think about musicians responding to accusations that their music influenced someone in a negative way. Do you see people assigning blame to others? Think about politics. Do you see people creating elaborate disclaimers or explanations for their words and behaviors? Think about athletes using performance-enhancing drugs. What do you think when you see this happen? More important, do you do the same or do you accept full responsibility for yourself? God encourages you to be the kind of person that takes responsibility even when it's hard, knowing that you aren't alone—God is by your side.

WHAT IS IT?

God's Will

"For I know the plans I have for you," declares the LORD, "plans to prosper you and not to harm you, plans to give you hope and a future." Jeremiah 29:11 NIV

Donovan was thrilled to land a job at his local supermarket. The hours were good, and the pay was pretty great too. As part of his training, he was encouraged to hone his customer-service skills. It was expected that the cashiers begin their customer interaction with courtesy.

"Hello, sir [or ma'am]. Did you find everything you were looking for today?"

"Yes, thank you."

"Did you have any coupons before I ring this up?"

"No, unfortunately I don't. Thank you for asking."

If the cashier happens to be a high school student, questions gravitate in that direction. If the customer knows the cashier or, worse, the cashier's family, the questions become more specific. If that customer knows the cashier is a junior or senior, then the questions can become predictable.

"What are you going to do after high school? Are you going to college? What college will you attend? What will you study?"

Everyone in Donovan's small town knew his family. Being a senior is difficult enough. Feeling pressure to make a decision about the future from your family, friends, and teachers is expected but annoying. Experiencing that pressure from near strangers ranks even lower on the enjoyment scale.

"Honestly, sir [or ma'am], I haven't decided yet," Donovan would reply, and if it were someone from his church he might add, "but I'm trying to find God's will." It seemed to deflect the questions.

After the winter break of Donovan's senior year, he began to feel the pressure of the questions more acutely, even to the point that he worried it might be causing him an ulcer. He had a sour ache in the pit of his stomach. Donovan began to consider a variety of the traditional options: community college, state school, a vocational school, and the military. At church, he continued to hear his fellow seniors mention God's will.

 FAITH UNPLUGGED:

The plans that God has for your life are amazing. Don't forget they begin with who you are. Who you are will always be more important than what you do.

Donovan began to suspect that as a Christian this concept was something he should consider not just something to use as a convenient response to inconvenient questions.

He didn't know exactly how to approach the subject, so he looked first to the Bible. Donovan found that Jesus instructed people to do God's will, which didn't clear things up for him. In Acts and Romans, Paul mentioned going or not going to different places because of it. In addition, he learned that it had to do with renewing his mind; he should do it from his heart.

Well, he thought, *that was about as clear as mud*. Donovan determined he should ask somebody. His friend Tatum served as a student leader in the youth group at the church Donovan had started attending last fall. He had known Tatum for a long time and trusted her, and he figured Tatum was his best candidate for information. It also didn't hurt that he always thought she was kind of cute.

"Hey, Tatum, wait up," Donovan yelled down the hall.

Tatum saw Donovan over her shoulder and stopped to wait. When Donovan pulled up, she gave him a warm smile. "What's up, Donovan?"

"I have a question about God that I thought you might be able to answer."

"Sure. What's your question?" she asked as the two made their way to a nearby bench outside the school.

"How do I find out God's will?"

"Oh, man," Tatum said, laughing. "Everyone seems to have a different idea of what it means to 'be in God's will.'"

"So I'm not alone in this," Donovan said.

"Nope. Not at all. But I remember Pastor Steve talking about it, and basically I remember this. You can see God's will in two areas. He said there is God's general will, which includes things like wanting everyone to know him and follow his instructions," Tatum began.

"That would be like loving your neighbor, right?"

"Exactly! And the second area was God's specific will, which is more personal for each individual. Pastor Steve mentioned a few Scriptures that talk about how God has a plan for our lives."

"That's good to hear, but also a little scary. I mean, what happens if I totally miss God's will?" Donovan asked.

"I feel that way too sometimes. I just keep trying to remember that it's not all up to me. God wants to reveal his will for our lives to us, and we just need to seek him out and be open."

"Do you think God could be the reason I'm good at science?"

"Yeah, absolutely! Since he made you that way, it might have something to do with your future. The things that we love, that we're good at, and that we dream about—I think they all come into play. Oh, and the other thing he talked about was that we have to remember that God doesn't ask us to accomplish his will alone. He is with us, as are the people he brings into our lives."

"That's actually really reassuring. So," Donovan said with a smile, "like I said, how do I find out his will?"

"I don't think there's some simple three-step process. We already talked about paying attention to our likes, skills, dreams, and stuff like that. And praying is always good. And sometimes I ask people, like my parents and Pastor Steve, what they think. And we want to make sure we're being wise. Like, we don't want to make a decision solely based on finances, but we should consider it. I'm sure there are other things too. You could always talk to Pastor Steve about it. He loves this topic. Does that help?"

"Tatum, it helps a ton. I appreciate it." He gave her a quick hug.

"I'm glad I could help," she said with a surprisingly flirtatious smile.

 ## FAITH LINK:

Jesus, I know that you have a plan and purpose for my life. Guide me in that direction. I want your way and not my own. Along the way, help me to remember that the most important thing is the person I'm becoming in you.

 ## POWER UP:

Do you realize that God has an amazing plan and a specific purpose for your life? He has invited you into his revolution of love in the world, and he wants to use you to make the world a better place to live. There are specifics to his plan, but he cares much more about the general aspects. The general aspects involve YOU! He wants desperately to save you, love you, forgive you, heal you, restore you, teach you, guide you, protect you, and provide for you. In addition, he wants to transform you into the person he originally designed and created you to be. He wants you to become the kind of person who loves, cares, listens, supports, serves, obeys, thanks, remains pure, and lives so well that people take notice. He has an amazing life destined for you to live. It's a life better than you could ever imagine. It's life's greatest adventure. Allow him to renovate your soul and guide you to your destiny.

DOES IT EXIST?

Truth

DOWNLOAD:

Jesus answered, "I am the way and the truth and the life. No one comes to the Father except through me." John 14:6 NIV

Stuart and Mason met the first week of school when they saw each other wearing the same Vintage Vantage T-Shirt. Stuart was a junior, and Mason was a freshman who had just moved into town. The two hit it off quickly, discovering that they had a lot in common. They listened to the same bands, enjoyed the same kind of movies, and were unashamedly addicted to the same computer games. Stuart remembered how lonely his freshmen year felt, so he took Mason under his wing.

Stuart introduced Mason to all of his friends. He provided Mason with all the information he needed to avoid public humiliation. In addition, since Stuart had a car, he ended up chauffeuring Mason to every school event. As they became better friends, they started hanging out periodically at a bagel place near the school.

The friendship took a giant leap forward when Mason discovered that Stuart was a Christian. Growing up in a nonreligious home had left Mason with lots of questions. Eventually Mason made a decision to become a follower of Jesus as well. Their bagel stops became a weekly Saturday-morning ritual that combined bagels with Bible study, prayer, and fellowship. Those meetings continued for two years until Stuart left to study philosophy and religion at a renowned university. Stuart wavered between becoming a minister or a college professor, so the double major made sense.

Stuart was going to be back in town for spring break, and he contacted Mason to schedule a reunion at the bagel shop. Mason showed up five minutes early on Saturday to grab their usual booth in the back. When he arrived, Stuart was already there.

"Hey, Stuart! It's good to see you. I see we both had the same idea," Mason said as Stuart stood. They shook hands somewhat formally.

"We need our booth. It's tradition," Stuart proclaimed with a smile. The two friends left their jackets and walked to the counter.

"It's so good to see you, man!" Mason exclaimed again.

"I'm sorry I've been so bad about keeping in touch," Stuart responded.

"That goes for me, too," apologized Mason.

"I guess we have a lot of catching up to do."

"Definitely. I have so much to tell you, but I want to hear all about you first."

"Can I help you?" asked the cashier.

"I'll take a blueberry bagel with honey-nut cream cheese and a coffee. My friend will have a ..." Stuart said, turning to Mason.

"The same, please," Mason said to the clerk, "except with blueberry cream cheese." He turned to Stuart. "You sure you got this?"

"You bet. It's my treat."

"Thanks!"

They returned to their booth and Mason started filling Stuart in on all the high school happenings. He concluded by sharing about how he felt he'd grown in his relationship with Jesus. He began to notice that Stuart was growing distant, communicating either disinterest or discomfort. Mason wasn't sure what was wrong but didn't press the issue.

"I'm glad to hear things are going well for you, Mason. That's awesome. You've come a long way since you we met. I'm proud of you," Stuart affirmed.

"Thanks, but enough about me. What's going on with you, college man? How's college life?" Mason asked.

"I love it. It's not quite what I expected, but I really am enjoying myself."

"What didn't you expect?"

"There were a lot of things I guess I wasn't ready for. I didn't expect my schedule to be so different. It was a bit of an adjustment to get used to not having class every day, one right after another. I have a lot more free time, but at the same time, there's a lot more work. I can't even tell you how much I've had to read this year."

"You like reading, though, so that has to be kind of cool, right?" Mason inquired.

"Definitely. I love reading, but still! It's been really challenging."

FAITH UNPLUGGED:

Truth does exist, and all truth finds its roots in God. God is truth, and all truth comes from him.

"Do you mean it's been challenging to keep up with your classes or challenging to your beliefs?" Mason asked, spying an open door.

"Both. There's so much to read," Stuart responded evasively.

Mason dug deeper. "How has it challenged your faith?"

"Honestly, it's hard to explain."

"Give me an example."

"You're not going to drop this, are you?" Stuart said, laughing.

"Nope." Mason gave his friend a challenging smile.

"All right. Let's take the idea of truth. I've always believed that the Bible is the final authority. All through high school, I used the Bible to argue against things like evolution or homosexuality. But after reading the philosophers and talking to my professors, I don't think I believe in an absolute truth anymore."

"What does that mean?" asked Mason.

"It means many things, I guess. For example, I just don't believe in the infallibility of Jesus or the Bible anymore. I think they provide one option for life and spirituality, but I don't think that it is the only way."

"Wow, Stuart. That's a major shift in just a few months."

"I know."

"Are you sure about all of this?"

"Well, pretty sure, yeah. It makes sense to me. Sorry to disappoint you."

"Dude, you don't disappoint me. Honestly, I'm just worried about you. It seems like you quickly swallowed a lot of stuff without really testing to see if it's true. I know I haven't read all the books or listened to all the lectures you have, but it seems rather dangerous to me."

"How is it dangerous?" Stuart asked.

"Well, for example, the statement that there is no such thing as absolute truth is contradictory. 'Cause it's an absolute statement. Second, if truth is relative, how do you explain things that all humans believe? For example, how do you explain that the majority of sane people agree that cold-blooded murder is wrong? Third, I think not believing in anything seems like a cop-out. If everything is relative, then no one can hold you accountable for the decisions that you make or the way they affect others. You can do whatever you want, whenever you want to do it. It seems dangerous to me."

"Mason, that was a pretty impressive answer. I'll think about it, but, well, you haven't taken all the classes and stuff I have."

"Well, OK. How about this? Come with me to church this Sunday. My pastor is doing a series on truth in relation to culture," Mason said.

"Sure, I'd like that. I'd like to hear what he has to say," Stuart replied thoughtfully.

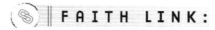

FAITH LINK:

Jesus, you are truth. There are so many contrary messages out there, so I need your help. Help me to accept, embrace, and proclaim truth. Teach me to think according to your ways and your words. Help me to stand for truth in a world that makes that so hard.

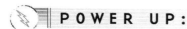

POWER UP:

Most of the academic or university world is a difficult place for Christians. A lot of Christian students enter college unprepared for the arguments and philosophies that they will be exposed to. They don't know what they believe or why they believe it. They have never researched the arguments against their faith in a life-giving environment that can guide them truthfully. Many have never learned to think critically about their faith or the ideas that attack it. Are you ready? Do you know what you believe and why you believe it? Have you learned how to think critically and logically? If not, seek the counsel of experienced, intellectual, and faithful Christians. Ask them to help prepare you. In addition, go to your local Christian bookstore and begin reading books that will help you in this area. Finally, continue to ask God to prepare your mind for action and to teach you how to test everything in accordance with his ways and words.

MOVING HOME

Family

DOWNLOAD:

Delighted with the world of things and creatures, happily celebrating the human family. Proverbs 8:31

"We're moving? Please tell me you're joking!" Ian cried.

"I'm sorry, Son. We don't have a choice. This is the best job I have ever been offered. Your father and I have agreed that this is what we need to do as a family," explained his mother.

Ian moaned. "I can't believe this is happening."

"Ian, we understand that this is a difficult decision. It wasn't easy for us, either," his father reminded him.

"Yeah, but at least you had a say in the process," he complained.

"Son," his father said. "That's enough."

"Dad, please. Do you realize what this means for me? I'm losing my whole life. You're moving me to a new city in a new state, where I don't even know anyone. There's no guarantee that I'll be able to make friends or play sports. Who knows if I'll even like the city or the school at all? I doubt it, and I know I won't like it as much as I like here," vented Ian as he stomped off to his room.

He returned to the kitchen an hour later. His parents were still there discussing how the move was affecting each of their children differently. It was obviously the hardest for Ian, the oldest, who interrupted, "When are we moving?"

"As soon as you finish school," his mother said gently.

"That's only two weeks away! Now you're telling me I'm going to have to spend the entire summer in a strange city with no friends? Arghhh!" Ian yelled and left the room, slamming every door behind him.

Ian told all of his friends the next day at school. He made plans with his best friend, Israel, to hang out that night to talk more about it. Iz handled the news as badly as Ian. He spent most of the day yelling at someone or in silent reflection, wondering what his life would be like without his closest confidant. In addition, Iz worried about Ian. As hard as it would be for him, it would be even harder to be the one who had to move away.

"I just can't believe this is happening," Iz stated as they walked into his room after school.

"I know. What are we going to do?" Ian was fishing for reassurance that their friendship would last.

"I wonder if my parents would let me come and visit you this summer for a couple of weeks. Then of course we have all the school breaks, the telephone, e-mail, IM, text-messaging, and, if we get really bored, snail mail." Iz attempted a chuckle. Ian breathed a slight sigh of relief at the reminder of their communications options.

A few minutes later, a thought hit Ian. "Aaahhh! I can't believe that I hadn't thought about this until now."

"What is it?" Iz asked, unsure whether to expect good news or bad.

"The only people I'll know in Austin will be my family. How am I going to survive being with them all summer with no escape?" he groaned. Iz didn't know what to say. It was a legitimate question. Ian's family was cool, but they didn't spend much time together. Ian interrupted Iz's thoughts. "You have to visit this summer. Do you understand me? You *have* to or I'm going to go crazy with those people!" He grabbed Iz's shoulders and was shaking him intensely when the two friends started laughing and punching each other.

The final two weeks of his sophomore year passed too quickly. Ian and Iz spent nearly every day together. They ate breakfast together before school and sat by each other during every lunch period. After school, the two friends spent their time visiting all their favorite spots one last time together as well as visiting everyone Ian could possibly want to see before becoming a Texan. In the evenings, they spent their time packing Ian's things, planning each school break, and reliving their six-year friendship. Suddenly, it was over. Moving day had arrived, and it was time for Ian to say good-bye to everything familiar, including Iz.

It was an emotional departure for everyone in the family. Ian, as expected, had the most difficult time. By the time they loaded everything into the two family vehicles and oversized moving truck and were on their way, he was exhausted. The family spent the next few hours in silence except for the requests for food and the bathroom. They grabbed a drive-through lunch and stopped for dinner, planning to spend the night along the way.

Dinner felt weird for everyone. It had been so long since all five members of the family ate together. Their last common meal happened at Easter, but even then, there were extended family members present. No one talked much, until Ian's younger brother spilled his drink all over the front of his shirt. He managed to miss his mouth entirely and looked shocked and confused. His expression lifted the gag order. The family spent the rest of the dinner listening to Mom and Dad retell embarrassing childhood stories about each of their children. They were laughing so hard that tears streamed down their faces. They laughed even harder when Ian's younger sister impulsively ran to the bathroom afraid that she might wet her pants from laughter. Everyone slept well that night, making the following day easier.

Ian and his family arrived in Austin the following afternoon. Driving through their new neighborhood to their new house created a sense of adventure and nostalgia. It was new and exciting. Everyone was pleasantly surprised when the car pulled into the driveway. Dad gave them the jaw-dropping grand tour of their new house. The house was by no means extravagant, but it was bigger and newer than their old house, and it exceeded their expectations. The highlight of the tour was Ian's discovery of a room designated for his drum set.

That night they unloaded most of the boxes and all of the furniture, so they could have something to sleep on. They spent the next day with everyone unpacking their individual belongings before moving to the common boxes. Ian and his mom unpacked the kitchen supplies while his siblings and his dad emptied the family-room boxes.

FAITH UNPLUGGED:

God created family before he created the church. Make your family a priority in your life as well.

"Hey, Mom, look what I found," Ian said, summoning his mom's attention; he was holding a box of uncooked spaghetti noodles. "Do you remember when we used to do spaghetti nights?"

"Of course I remember. We used to have them every Sunday night," his mom confirmed.

"And what day of the week is it today?" Ian teased, shaking the box.

His mom joined the kidding around. "Hmmm ... I'm going to guess that today is ... Sunday?"

"And what time of the day is it?"

"Hmm ... Now that's a tough question.... I'm going to guess ... about dinnertime?"

"Exactly," Ian said with a smile.

"Well, let's start cooking. Dig a pan out of that box over there for me. I'll get it started while you find enough plates for all of us."

An hour later, the family finished their second straight dinner together during which Ian's dad remembered another old family tradition. "Ian, do you remember what we used to do after spaghetti night?"

"Yep," Ian said with a grin.

His dad left the dining room and moments later returned, holding a box.

"Yahtzee! Dad, just like old times, you are going down! I own you at this game."

A half hour later, the family sat on the family-room floor, rolling dice and rolling in laughs. Ian smiled to himself as he remembered what their busy lives had caused them to forget—each other.

Later that evening he called Iz. "You know what?" Ian told Iz. "I think maybe, just maybe, this is going to be OK."

FAITH LINK:

Jesus, thank you for my family. It's so easy to take them for granted, ignore, or avoid them, but I don't want to do that anymore. Help me to make spending time with my family a priority in my life.

POWER UP:

How much time a week do you spend with your entire immediate family gathered in one place? How much time do you spend with each individual member? Do they spend a lot of time together without you? You aren't guaranteed to have the same friends in ten years. Chances are that in ten years you will have almost an entirely different group of close friends. Ten years after that, it could easily change again. The constant relationships in your life are your family. In ten or twenty years, they will still be your mom, dad, brother, or sister. Today, teens spend less time with adults and less time at home than ever before. It's unfortunate. Maybe your family isn't as fun or entertaining as your friends. Maybe your family is awkward or difficult to handle. Nevertheless, they are still family. Make time for them. Be creative. Include your younger siblings in your activities or errands. Ask your mom or dad if you can have a family meal together a few times a week. Take a day out of your week just to be at home. These steps will go a long way. Begin by taking a step this week.

RECYCLED LEADERS

Environment

DOWNLOAD:

God blessed them: "Prosper! Reproduce! Fill Earth! Take charge! Be responsible for fish in the sea and birds in the air, for every living thing that moves on the face of Earth."
Genesis 1:28

Elisa and Jared's school made a name for itself in the first few hours of the annual student-council leadership convention. The convention opened with an improvisational short-skit contest between three preselected schools, which included theirs. By the end of their skit, they were the clear and unanimous winners, bringing the entire audience to their feet in a boisterous standing ovation. As their improv team took their seats, they exchanged high fives and handshakes with all of the groups around them.

Several representatives from other schools asked to eat lunch with them. Elisa and Jared decided it was OK for the group to split up so that one or two members could sit with as many groups as possible. There would be plenty of time for them to eat together—they needed to cash in on their fame now. Besides, it would give them an opportunity to gather leadership ideas for next year.

Jared and Elisa stuck together and went to lunch with one of the few schools from a neighboring state.

"It's Freddy, right?" Elisa asked.

"That's right," the redheaded junior responded.

"Tell me a little about your student council. What do you guys do during the year?" Elisa probed. Jared and the young woman he was talking with turned their attention to Freddy.

"We do most of the normal stuff. We periodically meet with the principal or the school board when they have questions or we want to propose new ideas. Our stu-co also oversees all of the school dances. Homecoming and prom are the two biggest events. Of course we have to raise funds, and we hate that. One of the most unusual things that we do is coordinate the school's recycling program."

"Really?" Jared responded with a combination of excitement and surprise.

"How do you do that?" Elisa followed.

"Well, we started when recycling became mandatory in our town."

FAITH UNPLUGGED:

God has given the earth to humanity. He has entrusted his creation to our care. Do your part to care for the environment. It matters to him.

"Really?!" Jared's excitement and shock grew.

"Yeah, the city requires that each person separate their trash for recycling purposes. If you don't divide your garbage properly, the city will leave it. I guess you could say that our city is environmentally conscious," stated Freddy.

"That's really cool. How do you help with that?"

"The stu-co offered a few years ago to coordinate the recycling effort in the classrooms. We put some bins in each room—one for paper, another for plastic, a third for cardboard, and a fourth for miscellaneous items. There are regular trash cans, too, but the janitors take care of those. Every Monday morning about an hour before school, we all meet to collect the containers from the different rooms. We take them all to the room where all the Dumpsters are located and sort them into their appropriate big bins. The city takes care of the rest."

"Too bad our city doesn't require recycling," Jared said.

The other young woman, Tia, joined the discussion. "They might not require it, but they probably offer it. If you call the Public Works office, you can probably get something arranged."

"Are you serious?" Elisa asked.

"I can't guarantee it, but most cities recycle and are willing to work with schools and other larger organizations," added Freddy.

"That's not all we do," continued Tia. "Last year, we petitioned the school board to require the school to purchase recycled products whenever cost effective, and it passed. Also, as part of our fund-raising campaign, we started a small school-supply store where we sell as many recycled products as we can to students. This year we're hoping to coordinate with the city and the other schools to have a semiannual, city-wide cleaning day, where we pick up trash and stuff like that."

"Wow! You people are incredible. What made you so interested in environmental stuff?"

Tia spoke first. "I come from a proactive family. My parents have been concerned about the earth for years, so I grew up hearing about it. Then my freshman year I did a research paper on the environment, which really drove everything home for me."

"My church actually helped me develop my passion for the environment," claimed Freddy. "The church teaches that God entrusted his creation into our care. As a Christian, I believe that what we do with the things God gives us, including the earth, matters deeply to him and it should matter deeply to us. I guess those beliefs have turned into a genuine love for nature. I love being outdoors, and I want to do whatever I can to preserve its beauty."

"That is fascinating! I think we should talk to our stu-co about doing some of these things. What do you think, Jared?" Elisa asked.

"Definitely. Could we get your phone numbers and e-mail addresses in case we have any questions for you later?" Jared requested.

"Only if we can get yours as well," Freddy said with a wink. "We want to pick your brains too."

FAITH LINK:

Jesus, I stand in awe of your creation. When I see the oceans, the mountains, the stars, or the sunrise, I cannot help but think of you and wonder at your masterpiece. I want to appreciate it and enjoy it even more. Also, help me to realize that you entrusted this amazing place to your people and that you expect me to do my part to care for it.

POWER UP:

Should all Christians by nature be environmentalists? Granted, God does not want his followers to value trees more than they value people, but he does call his people to take conservation seriously. In the first book of the Bible, God instructs people to take care of his creation. He actually says that people are responsible for the earth, which means he will hold them accountable for what they do or don't do to his creation. What is your relationship with the environment? Are you being responsible with the way you live your life? Many people make excuses for not doing anything. Usually they consider themselves exempt because they believe the little difference they could make doesn't mean anything in the big picture. But if all of those people did their part, it would make a big difference. Find a way to get involved and bring other people with you. Pick up trash, recycle, and choose to buy recycled products when you can. Get creative and connect to the organizations in your community that are taking responsibility.

THE FORGOTTEN COMMAND

Busyness

DOWNLOAD:

Observe the Sabbath day, to keep it holy. Exodus 20:8

Two alarms rang around 6:00 a.m. across town from one another, awaking two teenagers—one guy and one girl. The snooze button looked so attractive after only five hours of sleep. Both debated the merits of hitting the snooze, but knew they could not. Time was already wasting away. Instead, both rolled out of bed, wiping the sleep from their eyes. Jordan walked to the kitchen to get food. Alexandra walked to the bathroom to get ready.

6:05–6:55 a.m.

Jordan poured himself a bowl of cereal and sat alone at the kitchen counter as the sun began to rise, bringing a light glow to the room. He had little time to eat, but he used it all, knowing that today would be like every other day. Upon finishing, he drank the leftover milk out of the bowl before putting his dishes away. Jordan stammered to the bathroom. He passed up a shower and simply washed his face and brushed his teeth. Picking up yesterday's jeans off the floor, he slid them back on, grabbed a T-shirt, laced his Converse All-Stars, and packed his backpack. Less than ten minutes later, he walked out the door to his car.

Alex hopped in the shower knowing she had little time. She rushed through washing and was out in ten minutes. Choosing an outfit and getting dressed happened quickly, so she could start on her hair. The clock made it clear there was no time to straighten, so today was a curly day. After finishing with her hair, she brushed her teeth and put on makeup. A final mirror check led to the packing of Alex's backpack. She collected two books from her desk, one from her nightstand, and one from under her comforter. Alex slid on her sandals and rushed outside to wait for her ride.

6:55–8:15 a.m.

Jordan pulled up to the curb; Alex jumped in the car. Last week, the show choir began practicing before school to prepare for their first performance and the upcoming competitions. They spent the drive to school discussing an English assignment between yawns and stoplights. When they arrived, they burst out of the car and sprinted to the auditorium. Mrs. Vanderbilt lacked tolerance for tardiness, even at seven. Jordan and Alex's four-minutes-late arrival drew a scornful glare, but they avoided a lecture. They sang and danced until the first bell rang.

8:15–9:05 a.m.

Jordan left the auditorium for history, where his group presented their portion of information on the Industrial Revolution. His teacher informed the class that there would be a test on all of the group presentations in two days.

Alex walked down the hall to geometry. After taking her desk, she immediately pulled out her daily assignment and checked it over one last time. The geometric proofs took much longer than she imagined last night. She learned a few new rules and wrote down tomorrow's assignment.

9:05–9:55 a.m.

Jordan and Alex rejoined for Spanish III, where *la profesora* gave them an oral vocabulary quiz. Jordan had a difficult time trilling his *r*'s, much to Alex's amusement. Next week, they would have an oral test that would count for 20 percent of their overall grade.

9:55–10:45 a.m.

It was Jordan's turn to survive geometry and the world of proofs. Alex took off from Spanish to anatomy. Thankfully, her teacher took her class to the library to give them time to research for their reports on the lymphatic system, which were due at the end of next week.

10:45–11:35 a.m.

Jordan's only happy thought throughout geometry was that woodworking class followed. Unfortunately, Alex headed from anatomy to chemistry. She loaded up on science classes due to her interest in pursuing a career in medicine. Chemistry was difficult, and the workload was astounding.

11:35 a.m.–12:05 p.m.

They devoured lunch while Jordan changed his English home-work based on the feedback Alex gave him earlier in the car. Alex complained about the length of their lunch period with a group of friends at a nearby table between bites.

12:05–12:55 p.m.

Jordan and Alex were in the same English class. Alex liked reading *The Scarlet Letter;* Jordan despised reading. They agreed that the daily discussion questions they had to answer and submit were overkill. This class always felt so long and tiring. It had something to do with their general lack of sleep and the presence of food in their stomachs.

12:55–1:45 p.m.

After English, Alex and Jordan could sense the school day approaching its end. They hoped the last two classes would take it easy on their homework. Apparently, their instructors didn't receive the memo. Jordan's biology teacher assigned another group project that required meeting outside of class. Alex's art class wasn't the relief she hoped it would be in her schedule. Her teacher dispersed another round of homework exercises.

1:45–2:35 p.m.
Jordan concluded his classes with speech during which his class drew dates for their ten-minute persuasive speech. He drew the following Tuesday. Alex ended the day with Western civilization and the joy of not having anything assigned for the following day.

FAITH UNPLUGGED:

God commands you to rest. Don't argue. Just do it.

2:35–5:40 p.m.
Jordan participated in cross-country after school. He generally liked running, but Coach made it hard to continue that trend. Alex spent her time practicing for the upcoming school play. The drama coach cast her in one of the lead roles.

5:40–6:00 p.m.
Jordan and Alex met at his car. They drove through Wendy's, taking advantage of the value menu. Jordan had only a few minutes to take Alex home before heading to work. Alex needed to get home to change clothes before leaving the house for a busy night of meetings.

6:00–10:30 p.m.
Jordan worked as a stock boy and bagger at the local grocery store. When he didn't have cross-country meets, he usually worked from six to close. The money went to covering the costs of his car payment, insurance, gas, cell phone, and occasional entertainment options.

Alex met a friend at six, who needed someone to talk to about her recent breakup. Around seven thirty, she dashed over to her church for choir practice. When they finished at nine, Alex ran a few errands for her mom in exchange for using her car. She also stopped by her boyfriend's house for thirty minutes. Since they attended different schools, they rarely saw each other and Alex didn't want to go a third night without talking.

10:30 p.m.–1:15 a.m.

By the time Jordan and Alex returned home, they were worn out from the day. Each of them spent a few minutes talking to their parents, who were finishing their day's work as well. At a quarter till eleven, they unpacked their books for another night of homework. Both of them knew that tomorrow night would be even busier, so they needed to try to work ahead in geometry and English.

1:15 a.m.

They set their alarm clocks to ring at six o'clock. Their Bibles rested on their nightstands; they looked at them for a second before turning out the lights. Jordan's and Alex's minds raced about the work they didn't finish, the friends they didn't see, and the projects they hadn't started. Two minutes later, their exhaustion took over as they fell hard asleep. Tomorrow night they would do the same.

FAITH LINK:

Jesus, I live in a world that moves so fast. It's a world that tells me the busier I am, the more important and valuable I am. You, however, say that my worth and value were determined by you a long time ago. You confirm that my value is not dependent on what I do but who you are and the worth you gave me. Help me to remember that. Help me to stop, to rest, to take time out of my day for you.

POWER UP:

Out of the Ten Commandments that God gave Moses, there is one that American Christians seem to have forgotten. It's the command to take a day off work. The command is to rest. Is your life too busy? Are you tired all the time, yet always behind on getting things done? Did you ever think about taking a mandatory day off every week? Your first response is probably wondering how you're going to finish in six days what you can't in seven. What would happen if you said no to some things? What would happen if you dropped a couple of things from your schedule so you could fit everything within six days? You think you have to do all of these things, but you don't have to do them. You think that being busy means you are important or valuable, but you're wrong. All being busy does is make you tired, cranky, and miserable. It definitely doesn't make you happy or healthy. God put resting in the Top Ten for a reason. He knows how important it is to stop and remember where our value comes from. He knows it's important to stop, think, sleep, pray, rest, and enjoy. Step out of the cycle of busyness. Rest and find God in ways you never imagined.

INFLUENZA

Leadership

⏬ DOWNLOAD:

Love and truth form a good leader; sound leadership is founded on loving integrity. Proverbs 20:28

It was Monday morning when Luis heard the page on the intercom: "Luis Stevens, please report to the principal's office. Luis Stevens to the principal's office. Thank you."

Luis's buddies pointed at him and broke out in a chorus of "uh-ohs." As he rose from the cafeteria table to head for the all-too-familiar office, their clamor attracted the attention of half the student body. About three months ago, Luis was summoned to the office while he was in Spanish class. He was asked by the principal and guidance counselor to explain his actions during the junior class's career-day field trip. Luis and two of his friends had apparently embarrassed the guidance counselor by talking during the seminar on career opportunities.

Two weeks ago, Principal Stewart discovered a copy of an "Even Stevens" betting sheet that Luis accidentally left on the school's copier. "Even Stevens" was the name of the loose underground gambling ring Luis ran for fun. Each participant forked over five dollars a week to play in a winner-takes-all college and professional sports pool. He produced a sheet with the matchups, and each participant circled who they thought would win and chose the total number of points scored in the game of the week for a tiebreaker. Luis inherited the pool from an upperclassman two years before, and quite a few teachers were involved. Nevertheless, Mr. Stewart wasn't too impressed and shut it down.

Luis sauntered down the hall wondering what he could have possibly done this time. *OK, I shut Even Stevens down. I haven't been on any field trips. Last time I checked, my grades are decent and all my teachers are cool with me. I know I haven't done anything major. What could this possibly be about?*

Despite a few missteps, Luis was not a troublemaker. He never intentionally disrespected anyone. As a student, he maintained a B average, and he participated in a couple of extracurricular activities, experiencing some success. Except for the occasional funny stunt that his friends pulled him into (it was always their idea), he rarely even said much. Generally, he was described as a good student, quiet, and respectful with mischievous friends and an attraction for the edge of innocence.

Luis entered the office apprehensively and then spoke quietly. "You paged me?"

"Hey, Luis! Mr. Stewart wanted me to set up an appointment with you for later on this week. He wanted to know when the best time for you would be."

"I guess anytime. I don't have a lot going on this week," Luis responded slowly.

"How about meeting tomorrow during your fourth hour?"

"That works for me. I guess I'll see you then," Luis agreed, and then turned to walk to his next class.

During his Tuesday-morning classes, Luis found himself worrying about the approaching meeting. His friends enjoyed watching him squirm and added their own commentary. Their ideas centered on Luis taking the blame for something they did.

Finally, fourth hour on Tuesday rolled around. Luis walked slowly down the hall toward the office while his friends walked to class. He passed a few of them in the hallway. They wore black and carried hankies, pretending to mourn the loss of their friend. Normally, Luis would have found it hilarious, but it did little to calm his nerves. When he finally arrived, the principal was waiting with his door open.

"Mr. Stevens, come on in," he said from behind his massive desk. "Please shut the door behind you."

That can't be good, Luis thought.

"Have a seat, Luis. How have you been?" Principal Stewart inquired.

"Good, sir. Everything seems to be going well."

The two engaged in small talk for a few minutes, while inwardly Luis was squirming. The principal obviously knew every one of Luis's friends and activities because he asked about them all. Eventually, he moved on to the reason he wanted to meet with Luis.

"Well, Mr. Stevens, I'm glad to hear that everything is going well for you. I'm sure by now you're wondering why I called you in here today. It's not very often that I call a student in just to chat."

"Yeah, I didn't think you did." Luis felt a fine sweat break out.

"Luis, I wanted to ask you to do me a favor."

Surprised but relieved, Luis blurted out, "Sure, anything! Well, within reason ..." he added, his voice trailing off.

"I want you to consider running for student-council president."

"What?" he said. "You're kidding, right?"

"No, I'm serious. I think you would do a great job."

"Mr. Stewart, no offense, but I'm not the leader type."

"What do you mean 'not the leader type'?"

"I'm just not a leader."

"Luis, you're one of the most effective leaders in this entire school."

"I'm really not." Luis's confusion reached a new level as he began to build an argument while Mr. Stevens continued.

"I know you've never been in a leadership position before ..."

Luis checked that off his dispute list.

"... but leadership is not about positions. Leadership is about influence, and few people have as much influence with students in this school as you do."

"Mr. Stewart—" Luis began before the principal interrupted.

"Luis, I know exactly what you're going to say. You want to list the number of times you've been in trouble first. Then you'll list a bunch of other students who you think are more qualified. At some point, you'll talk about your friends, schedule, and lack of experience before closing with the observation that you don't think you influence anyone. The problem is that none of your arguments explains what I see. For example, those friends of yours would be getting into a lot more trouble if you were not a part of their group. I know I made you shut down Even Stevens, but you did have over a hundred students and faculty involved if my sources are correct. Quite impressive. I could keep going, but I'm not going to do that to you."

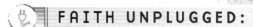

FAITH UNPLUGGED:

The biggest difference between leaders and followers is that leaders take responsibility for the influence they exert.

Luis sat, stunned. Principal Stewart really had done his homework.

"I'm not asking you for an answer today. Think about it. Talk to your friends and family. Take this application, and if you're interested, bring it back here by Friday."

Luis walked out of the office as slowly as he walked into it. A few minutes later, his friends all found him and berated him with questions. Finally, Luis spoke.

"He asked me to run for student-council president," he whispered.

"Are you serious?"

"Yeah."

"Dude, that's awesome. You would make the best president ever!" responded his buddies.

"Guys, think about it. I'm not cut out for this."

"Whatever, Luis. You're perfect for this and you'll win the election in a landslide."

"Get real. Even if I did run, I wouldn't win," Luis corrected.

"You get real. I'm telling you. You're a shoe-in. If you don't believe me, give it a shot. What have you got to lose if you won't win?"

"All right, I'll do it."

Four weeks later, the student body appointed Luis Stevens as their new student-body president. He won by an unprecedented margin. He thought he was scared before. Nothing prepared him for this feeling, yet at the same time, everyone seemed to believe in him more than he believed in himself. *Maybe,* he thought, *I can do this.*

 FAITH LINK:

Jesus, the world has never seen a better leader than you. Teach me to lead by setting an example of loving integrity and service. Help me to take responsibility for the influence you have given me whether I am in a position of leadership or not.

POWER UP:

Most people think that all leaders look, act, and talk a certain way. They will tell you that some people are born leaders and others are not. Nothing could be further from the truth. Sure, some people might naturally be more gifted at public speaking, organization, delegating, brainstorming, or raising support, but that does not necessarily make them good leaders. If you judge leaders according to their giftedness, then Adolf Hitler was one of the world's greatest leaders. God does not judge a good leader by talent, but by character, service, integrity, responsibility, goodness, and love. The world's best leaders are those who humbly accept the influence God has given them with the people in their lives and faithfully serve in love. God rewards those who are faithful with more influence. Where do you have influence? Are you accepting responsibility for that? Are you faithfully serving with loving integrity and service? If so, remain faithful, for God is smiling on you. If not, begin to do so and watch your life become enriched.

CRASH AND BURN

Failure

DOWNLOAD:

No matter how many times you trip them up, God-loyal people don't stay down long; Soon they're up on their feet, while the wicked end up flat on their faces. Proverbs 24:16

Sophomore Hayden Masters was the first student in school history to qualify for the state science fair. Hayden constructed a model of a magnetically levitated train based upon an electrically produced Meissner-like effect. The sound of the idea alone impressed everyone who heard about it. When the train actually worked, Hayden became somewhat of an icon. He achieved a cool status rarely given to those whose passions are academic. That status rose when he placed third in the state competition. His grandiose finish landed him on the front page of not only the school newspaper, but the city's as well. In addition, the administration held a special school assembly to honor his achievement.

"It's my honor on behalf of River Valley High to present you, Mr. Hayden Masters, with this plaque signifying your third-place finish in the state science fair. This plaque will go on permanent display next to your award in the school's display case. We will make sure we leave plenty of room for next year. Again, congratulations."

It was after the principal's speech that the pressure began. When the assembly ended, Hayden felt the book close on that year's project, and all of his science-oriented conversations were directed toward next year's idea.

"So, Hayden, any ideas for next year?"

"What have you got cooking for next year's fair?"

"You're only going to be a junior next year, which means you have a legitimate chance at winning the competition two years in a row. Has anyone ever done that before?"

"Legitimate chance? It's more like a guarantee. Who's going to beat this guy? He's a science-fair machine. No one else should even bother entering for the next two years. They might as well just hand you the award."

After a few weeks, the conversations steadily decreased as the student body moved on to the next big thing, which always happens. Hayden enjoyed moving out of the spotlight. He attempted to return to his normal routine, but it felt different. Even though the spotlight was off, he still felt the pressure to perform. The days were counting down until next year's fair, and the expectations ran much higher. He knew everyone assumed a first-place finish. He also knew that in the world of science there are no guarantees.

Days turned into weeks. Weeks turned into months. Spring turned into summer. Summer became fall, and Hayden became a junior. He exhausted the school's science offerings during the first semester, so second semester he would have to begin taking classes from a university online or concurrently enroll at the local community college. Word spread quickly around school that in the spring Hayden Masters would study college-level science. This news, coupled with the science fair inching closer, refueled the conversations and increased the pressure.

"Science fair is coming. I can't wait to see what you got this year, Masters."

"Hayden, can I interview you in the next couple of weeks? I'm putting together a pre-science-fair piece for the school newspaper to educate students on all that the science fair entails."

"Hayden," said one of his science teachers, "I'm still waiting on that idea of yours. Let me know if you need any help deciding."

"We were thinking about putting some science-fair banners up in the hallway. Do you like 'Hayden Masters the Universe'? It's kind of a play on that old He-Man cartoon."

The pressure mounted as each day passed, but it was familiar. Hayden lived with high expectations of himself. His family did the same. The Masters family formed a long line of overachievers. Though none of his siblings garnered this much attention, his older brother and sister had enrolled in prestigious universities. His brother studied mechanical engineering while his sister studied biomedical chemistry. Hayden's father was a well-known surgeon, while his mother ran her own real-estate business from home.

It was a loving family, but everyone understood what it meant to be a Masters.

Hayden debated numerous ideas. He considered venturing into the world of physics by exploring thermodynamics. The project would examine if light bulbs filled with different gases glow more or less brightly. He also thought about taking a stab at chemistry by testing how the level of chlorine affects carbon filters used in fighting environmental pollution. In the end, he decided to stick with engineering. No other project was as flashy as building a hovercraft for three adults. The idea lived up to the expectations, mainly because every student knew what a hovercraft was and secretly wanted one as a child.

"You're going to build a hovercraft! That's amazing. Can I be one of your test participants?"

"That's incredible. I can't believe you can actually build a hovercraft."

"Sweetness. Can I have it when you're done?"

The only hesitation came from a couple of his science teachers who thought the idea was great, but they had seen it done before. It lacked originality and didn't explore a deeper aspect of science than the previous year. He considered their insights and made a few modifications that impressed them. Of course, the adjustments would take quite a bit more work, but he had a reputation to uphold.

A month later, Hayden carried his project into the convention center, set everything up for the fair, and began waiting on the judges. While the judges worked their way around, Hayden took notice of the competition. Two other students entered hovercrafts, which worried him at first. Then he noticed that one didn't work, and the other not only lacked the changes he had introduced, but also could hold only one adult. The biggest surprise of the event was the increase in the number of contestants from last year. Hayden estimated an extra thirty or so participants from various schools, which would make it more difficult to be one of the five projects the judges picked to advance.

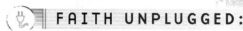

FAITH UNPLUGGED:

How you respond to failure is much more important than whether or not you fail.

As the day progressed, Hayden's nerves went on a roller-coaster ride. The longer it took the judges to make it around the room, the more he figured they had to consider. In other words, there were better projects than last year. However, the continual crowd around his booth kept him encouraged and upbeat. He had to begin regulating rides on the hovercraft. The visitors rode it so much that he wondered if it would hold up for the rest of the day.

Finally, the judges made it to his stand. Hayden recognized a few of them from last year and vice versa. He spent a few minutes eloquently explaining the hovercraft and the scientific principles involved before inviting three of the five judges to hop on for a ride. The looks on their faces communicated that they were impressed and enjoying themselves. His confidence soared as he waited a few hours for the results.

"Attention, everyone. Attention," one of the judge's voices echoed over the PA. "Thank you all so much for coming to this year's district science-fair competition. Before I announce the five state-qualifying contestants, I want to tell you all how difficult you made our jobs as judges today. I have been doing this for years and I have never seen a collection of projects like we have assembled here today."

His speech was interrupted by the applause of numerous parents, science teachers, and various other guests and participants. As the sound lessened, the judge restarted, "Now the moment you've all been waiting for. This year's state qualifiers are Whitney King, Javier Mendes, Andrea Chang, Chance Bishop, and Fabian Rice. Congratulations and again thank you to all the participants."

Hayden did a double take. *Maybe those were just the runners-up*, he speculated. But a cold sweat formed on his forehead as he realized his hovercraft had not even placed. Suddenly the frustration of the past few months caught up with him. Accompanied by a torrent of screams and a few choice words that surprised even him, Hayden began smashing his science project, until it hardly resembled the machine he'd brought in only hours before.

FAITH LINK:

Jesus, I hate failing, especially when I try so hard. It's so difficult not to take it personally. I feel like because I have failed that I'm now a failure, but I know it's not the same thing. Everyone fails—that is why we so desperately need you to be our Savior. At the same time, I want to do my best for you, so please help me to get back up and try again.

POWER UP:

Have you ever failed to meet your expectations? Have you ever failed to live up to the expectations of others? Do you remember how it felt? Do you remember how you responded? People respond to failure in different ways. Some simply give up and never try again. Others find themselves emotionally crushed. It's so easy to attach your value to your achievements, especially in a performance-driven world. It's even easier to want to give up, throw in the towel, or quit and never come back to something that you were unsuccessful at. Just because you failed does not make you a failure. Failure only happens when you quit completely. Otherwise, it was a failed attempt, and the next one might be the one that works. If you feel like you keep failing at something, don't give up. Keep trying while seeking help from God and others. Guard your heart to make sure you enjoy what you're doing in the process. Stay diligent but also lighthearted and humble. If you feel like you have already quit, it's never too late to try again!

OPEN INVITATION

Salvation

DOWNLOAD:

Everything that goes into a life of pleasing God has been miraculously given to us by getting to know, personally and intimately, the One who invited us to God. The best invitation we ever received! 2 Peter 1:3

"Cedric, I would like you to meet Stu. He will be your student guide for the rest of the day. Welcome to Kennedy High. Have a great first day," Mr. Dickinson said as the two students shook hands. "He's all yours, Stu."

"Thanks, Mr. Dickinson," Stu replied as the principal walked back into his office. Stu served on the student council, and showing new students around school was part of his job. "Well, Cedric, welcome to Kennedy. Where are you from?"

"My mom and I just moved into town from Portland."

"What brought you to Minneapolis?"

"I guess my mom wanted a fresh start or something like that."

"That's cool. Do you have a copy of your schedule? We can start walking to your first class while we talk."

"Sure, here it is."

Leading the way down the hallway, Stu commented, "English with Miles, not a bad way to start the day. Mrs. Miles is cool. She's obsessed with Shakespeare, but I think that's a requirement for all English teachers." Cedric laughed, which eased Stu's nerves slightly.

"Here it is. I'll introduce you to Mrs. Miles, then I have to run off to computer class. Wait for me right here after class, and I'll show you to your next stop."

Stu assisted Cedric all day, answering as many questions as he could while making it a point to introduce Cedric to his friends. At the end of the day, Cedric expressed his gratitude. "Thanks a lot, Stu. I appreciated the help today. Maybe I'll see you around tomorrow?"

"Absolutely. If I don't see you in the morning, find me at lunch. I'll be in the same area. I can introduce you to a few more people and answer any more questions."

"Sweet. I'll see you then," Cedric affirmed as the two parted ways.

Over the next couple of weeks, Stu continued to check in on Cedric. He gave him the rundown on all of his teachers, filled him in on the social scene, and provided him with all of the necessary warnings he needed to avoid public humiliation. Cedric adjusted quickly to Kennedy life, settling into a rhythm, joining a club, and beginning to make a friend or two.

On Friday after school, Stu stood outside talking with a bunch of his friends about their weekend plans. He noticed Cedric sitting on the curb apparently waiting for a ride. Stu swiftly finished the planning session and joined Cedric on the curb.

"What's up, Cedric?" he exclaimed as he sat down.

"Hey, Stu!" Cedric responded, surprised to see him.

"Are you waiting for a ride?"

"Yeah, my mom called. She has to stay a little later at work than usual, so I get to hang here for a while."

"Can you reach your mom on the phone?"

"Yeah, why?"

"Give her a call. Tell her you found a ride home," Stu said, smiling and standing to his feet.

"Are you sure? I can wait. It's no big deal."

"Come on. Make the phone call. It's no problem. I don't have anything to do for the next few hours anyway."

On the way to Cedric's house, Stu invited Cedric to join his friends for pizza and a movie that night at his house. He even offered to pick Cedric up and take him home if he needed the ride. Cedric took him up on the offer. Stu and Cedric didn't have a lot in common, but Cedric appreciated the uncommon effort Stu made toward a friendship. Cedric didn't know too many people like Stu.

After that Friday, Stu attempted to find Cedric every day after school to see if he needed a ride home. Periodically, he did. They didn't hang out many times outside of school, but the few times Cedric was free, Stu invited him along with whatever he had happening. Cedric figured his novelty as the new student would wear off and Stu's kindness would disappear with it. It never did. It was annoying, comforting, and intriguing.

What is this guy's deal? Cedric thought. He decided to pay closer attention to Stu to unlock the mystery. After all, no one was that nice without having an agenda. Cedric observed Stu around school. He listened more intently when someone mentioned Stu's name. When appropriate, he asked a couple people what they thought of Stu. In general, everyone liked him. Only a few people had anything negative to say. Cedric deduced that some of their comments were rooted in jealousy, others in a difference of beliefs.

Another day after school, Stu tracked Cedric down. Cedric tried to avoid him just to test how far Stu was willing to go.

"Hey, Cedric, I've been looking for you. How was your day?"

"Sorry about that. It was a decent day, though."

"Nice. I wanted to see if you needed a ride home."

"That'd be great," Cedric said, thinking that maybe he should just ask Stu to explain himself. The ten-minute ride home was as good a time as any to ask.

After the two entered Stu's jeep and exchanged small talk, Cedric threw out his question.

"Stu, what's your deal?"

"What do you mean?"

"I mean you're kind of strange," Cedric opened. "I don't understand why you've been so nice to me or why you seem to be so nice to everyone. You smile all the time, but I know from asking a few other students, you haven't had an easy life. From what I can tell, you don't party, you don't sleep around or cuss, but you don't judge others who do. I have never met anyone else like you, so I want to know what makes you so different."

"Do you really want to know?" Stu asked.

"I wouldn't have asked otherwise."

"The short answer is that I'm a Christian."

"Whatever. You are not." Cedric laughed, assuming Stu was joking.

"No, seriously, I am."

"Oh," Cedric said, astonished. "Well, you're not like other Christians that I've met."

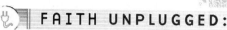

FAITH UNPLUGGED:

Through Jesus, God is inviting you into a beautiful life with him.

"I'm sorry to hear that," Stu answered before continuing, "I became a follower of Jesus a few years ago. I don't have a dramatic story to tell you. I've been through some hard times, but who hasn't? I grew up in church, but I ignored most of it until my freshman year. I was exploring spirituality at the time for some reason. For the first time, I seriously considered Jesus' life and teachings. I wrestled with it for a long time. In the end, I accepted him. He honestly changed my life. I can't explain it really. I didn't have this big experience where everything transformed instantly. It was slower and subtler. Eventually, I fell in love with God and, in turn, with people. I guess you can say I dedicated my life to love."

Stu sounded authentic. Cedric had heard people talk about their relationship with God before, but this was different. It sounded like something he would actually want to have as well. "Stu, that's really cool. I've talked to Christians before, but it's different with you. It's more than just believing it—you actually live it. I wish I could do that."

"You actually can," Stu answered rapidly, catching Cedric by surprise. "The way of Jesus is an open invitation to everyone, including you. It doesn't matter where a person comes from or what they have done, Jesus accepts and forgives everyone who comes to him. He taught through his life, death, and resurrection that anyone could find salvation and enter into a better way of living. Jesus waits on us to accept his invitation and openly enter into a relationship with him that mysteriously changes us from the inside out. Cedric, you can begin that relationship anytime you want."

"If I wanted to start it now, how would I do that?"

Stu pulled the Jeep into a parking lot. "It begins with prayer, which is really talking to God."

"What do I say?" Cedric asked.

"Why don't we pray together? I'll help you out by praying, and you repeat each sentence after me. Is that cool?"

"That would be awesome," Cedric exclaimed as the two young men began to pray.

FAITH LINK:

Jesus, I believe you are who you say you are. I believe that you lived, died, and came back to life. You are the only one who can forgive my sins and restore my soul. Please enter my life, change me on the inside, and teach me to live in a real relationship with you. Thank you for inviting and accepting me into your kingdom.

POWER UP:

As you have read this book, you have seen a glimpse of God's love for you and his invitation into a new life. If you have tried living your life apart from him, you realize that it doesn't work. God designed you to experience life in a dynamic relationship with him. Your sins and mistakes have severed that relationship, breaking God's heart and filling your life with hurt, pain, confusion, and despair. God knew there was no way for you to repair the connection, so he took matters into his own hands. He sent his son, Jesus, to the earth to live a perfect life. Teaching people how to live in a renewed relationship with their creator, he died and returned to life to restore the relationship that sin and death had broken. Jesus invites you to turn from your way of living to the new life made possible in him. The way of Jesus is the best way of living. Don't hesitate. The God who loves you is waiting to fill your life with hope, meaning, significance, and true life.

If you followed Jesus in the past but stopped and turned away, he continues to invite you back. No matter what has happened, he loves you and is still very capable of forgiving and restoring you. He has been waiting for you to return to him.

Whether you are ready to meet Jesus for the first time or want to come home to God, get involved at a local church. The journey of faith is impossible without the help, support, encouragement, prayers, and love of other Christians.

Welcome to that journey and a life of faith—unplugged.

TOPICAL INDEX

Additional copies of *Faith Unplugged for Guys* and
other Honor Books
are available from your local bookseller.

If you have enjoyed this book,
or if it has had an impact on your life,
we would like to hear from you.

Please contact us at:

Honor Books, Dept. 201
4050 Lee Vance View
Colorado Springs, Colorado 80918

Or visit our Web site:
www.cookministries.com

HONOR **HB** BOOKS

Inspiration and Motivation for the Seasons of Life